A RADICAL'S
RESPONSE
RAYMOND CROTTY

POOLBEG

A Paperback Original
First published 1988 by
Poolbeg Press Ltd.
Knocksedan House,
Swords, Co. Dublin, Ireland.

ISBN 0 905169 98 0

Cover design by Steven Hope
Typeset by Print-Forme,
62 Santry Close, Dublin 9.
Printed by The Guernsey Press Ltd.,
Vale, Guernsey, Channel Islands.

Contents

Preface

A referendum was held on 26 May 1987 to amend the Constitution so as to make it compatible with the Single European Act. That referendum was necessary because the government wished to implement the SEA as it stood rather than renegotiate it with the other member states of the European Economic Community; and the SEA as it stood had been found unconstitutional by the Supreme Court following reference to the Court by me. 324,977 people voted in the referendum against amending the Constitution. A further 1,337,977 chose not to vote or spoiled their votes. Only 755,425 voted for the amendment.

It has seemed right to me that I should explain to those who opposed amending the Constitution and to those who chose not to support the amendment my reasons for challenging the SEA in the courts. I do so in the hope that this explanation will confirm for them that in voting as they did, or in choosing not to vote, they acted in the best interests of the nation.

CHAPTER 1

From Flagstones to Fields

To Be a Farmer's Boy

Familiar situations can seem different when viewed from an unfamiliar perspective. Most social scientists are born into and live their lives in what the marketing people refer to as social classes A or B. I appear to be the only economist who has earned a living for a prolonged period - from 1942 to 1961 - solely from farming in a former capitalist colony. This is also the sole occupation of perhaps as much as one third of the world's workforce. That does not necessarily imply a clearer, truer view of society; merely a different one.

Entrance to economics via farming was itself largely influenced by the manner of my entry to farming. That was as part of a back to the land movement about which there has been more spoken and written than has been practised. Had I not been a town-bred farmer I would probably not have been an economist and certainly not the sort of economist that I am.

A "townie" becoming a farmer was not so out of the way in the Ireland of the 1940s. Most of the rest of the world was caught up in the Second World War. In neutral Ireland we had an Emergency. Life during the Emergency focussed mainly on the basics of defence and food. From the end of the "phoney war", in May 1940, invasion first by Germany and later by Great Britain seemed imminent. If the country was not invaded it might still go hungry; imports were virtually cut off. Tea was rationed to half an ounce per person per week and sugar to half a pound per person. White flour of 70% extraction was a memory of pre-war opulence and had been replaced by unpalatable brown bread of 95% extraction.

Circumstances of this nature sharpened the significance for an impressionable reader of geography texts that suggested that somehow poor Ireland always got it wrong, or at any rate this part of it did. Typical was the following table from Elenor Butler's *Geography Primer*.

Irish Foreign Trade 1936 (£s thousand)

EXPORTS		
	Twenty-Six Counties	Six Counties
Livestock	8,953	3,723
Food and drink	10,344	8,518
Textiles	269	25,148
Total exports	21,969	48,026
IMPORTS		
Total	39,913	51,618

Our exports of unprocessed, live animals were in value over twice those of the Six Counties; but our exports of processed foods were only a quarter more. We had nothing comparable to the North's great linen exports. When it came to imports, ours cost half as much more again as we earned from exports, leaving a large balance of trade deficit. Our neighbours, on the other hand, almost balanced their exports and imports. It was similar with other presentations of the Irish scene. If it was a list of "baddies", Ireland seemed always to head the list. If it was "goodies", Ireland just as certainly seemed to come last. Surely it need not be so? Could not Ireland, for example, produce somewhat fewer cattle and instead produce more wheat?

An early pig-keeping venture while I was still at school, though it did not confirm that revolutionising Irish farming and Irish geography were as simple or as profitable as Elenor Butler seemed to suggest, was not as disastrous as it might have been. It was based on feeding the waste bread from the family bakery to bonhamhs bought at Kilkenny fair. The legal requirement to incorporate 95% of the wheaten grain into the flour may well have caused more rather than less grain to be used during the Emergency, because the loaves of bread appeared to break so very easily. As a result, there was always an abundance of broken bread to feed to pigs in a hopelessly unbalanced and inappropriate diet. That casualties were not much worse was a tribute to the sturdiness of the Large White York pig of the day rather than to my husbandry. Apart from the occasional casualty, the cost of a diet of 100% broken bread was zero. Provided the pigs fattened, as they eventually did, a profit had to ensue.

Undeterred therefore by an experience of pig fattening which breached most of the canons of good husbandry, I was determined on matriculating from St. Kieran's College, Kilkenny in 1942 "to plough, to mow, to reap, to sow, to be a farmer's boy". Wiser counsels urged first a university degree, then, unlike now, a 'natural right' of any young person with parents able to pay the modest tuition and maintenance costs. But being a young man in a hurry to set about the wonderful things in Irish farming that the Department of Agriculture said could be both easily and profitably done, I rejected those wise counsels.

The USA by then was in the Second World War. Hitler was carving up the Russians and Rommel in North Africa was at El Alamein, only down the road from Suez. Britain and Belfast had been blitzed. The occasional German bomb was dropped on southern Ireland, including one on the North Strand in Dublin in 1941. I had gained reluctant parental consent to skip university and go to work for a farmer relative by using the utterly unfair bargaining point that the alternative would be à trip to His Majesty's recruiting office in Belfast to enlist in the RAF, as very many other Irish people were doing at the time. That exercise in filial blackmail expedited my passage from classroom to farm and from the flagstones of Kilkenny's streets to the fields of a county Kilkenny farm in the summer of 1942.

A year's farm work was followed by a year at the Albert Agricultural College, Glasnevin, which now houses a constituent college of the NIHE. "D'Albert", as it was commonly referred to, as well as being the principal teaching and experimental centre of the Agricultural Faculty of University College Dublin, had since its foundation given one-year courses designed to teach the rudiments of scientific

3

farming to young would-be Irish farmers. Frank Hussey was Housemaster at "d'Albert" in 1943-44 and for many subsequent years. A man of charm, wit and culture, he and Paddy McSweeney, my geography teacher at St. Kieran's College, were formative influences on my development during those years.

Unlike many other institutions in independent Ireland, 'd'Albert' retained its original title honouring the memory of the Prince Consort of Queen Victoria, who reigned at the time of its foundation. It did so for a very mundane reason. The pedigree boars from its long established pig herd were all named after the College as "Albert Prince this" and "Albert Prince that" and so on. Because to have dropped the name of Victoria's Consort from the College's title would have also necessitated its expurgation from the pedigrees of the boars, the college continued to be known as "d'Albert" to the end of its time as an agricultural establishment. *Sic transit gloria mundi*.

A year's sharecropping followed. I herded the cattle, made the hay and so on on an out-farm; and with a pair of horses cultivated the 20 or so acres of "compulsory tillage" on it. For my work I was to share the crop on the 20 acres. The experience was a useful introduction to the problems of farming.

The cropped land was second ley. That is, two years before it had been in pasture; and had been so for as long as anyone remembered. During the preceding year a crop of wheat and oats had been grown on it. Now wheat was to follow the oats and barley the wheat. As the old ley sod disintegrated during the second year of cultivation masses of centipedes, known as "red worms", were released to attack the roots of the growing grain crops. The damage done by the red worms to the plants was often compounded by crows tearing out the weakened plants to get at the worms feeding on the roots. Nowadays there is a spray to deal with this as with most infestations; but then there was nothing for it but continuous rolling of the land in an attempt to consolidate the very friable, decaying sod and impede the depredations of the red worm. The outcome, as I recollect, was a three way split of the crop: a third each to the red worms, to the land owner, and to myself.

4

A fine farm came on the market a month or so after the unconditional surrender of Japan to the Allied Powers on 9th August 1945. It comprised 204 acres of very good land in the District Electoral Division of Dunbell, some six miles east of Kilkenny town. Apart from 20 cropped acres, it was all under good pasture. This was very exceptional after the Emergency years of compulsory tillage. It was possible because the owner had another farm nearby where he had done most of his required tillage.

Learning the Hard Way

Unlike the First World War, agricultural prices had not risen greatly during the Emergency. This was mainly because the British Ministry of Supply, from the beginning of the war, became the sole buyer of Irish agricultural exports and held prices down. Land prices in Ireland reflected this cautious pricing policy. They were also influenced by recollections of the aftermath of the 1914-18 war, when many who had bought high priced land during the boom war years found themselves crippled with debt. Finally, there was the more immediate recollection of the "Economic War" of the 1930s, when the bottom fell out of the market for Irish agricultural produce. All of this combined to make it possible to buy in September 1945 in Dunbell, Co. Kilkenny, an excellent 204 acre farm for £5000. The price, which was considered high at the time, was less than one hundredth part of what similar land came to be worth thirty-five years later. If land was cheap it was because money was scarce. In my case the amount available was £3000, not an inconsiderable sum at a time when the average annual earnings of a worker were seventy-six shillings a week. It was possible to borrow a similar amount on mortgage. This was enough to pay auctioneers' and solicitors' fees and leave a very little to get through the first farming year.

The two extreme positions on the range of available options were a cautious or a high risk one. The cautious option was to rent out the 180 acres of grassland to an available, solvent tenant for £1000 a year. I could then concentrate on the

5

remaining twenty or so acres of tillage, making a living from that and using the conacre rent to clear the mortgage. The opposing alternative was to plough the whole farm for successive corn crops. With average yields, the guaranteed prices of the time would give a gross income of around £5000 per year. There was no difficulty for a young man in a hurry in making a choice.

Buying a tractor and rudimentary equipment on hire purchase, I ploughed the whole farm. Several well meaning, experienced persons attempted to dissuade me from a course that was directly contrary to current orthodoxy. Their advice boiled down to the warning that what I proposed to do had never been done previously and that it just would not work. I was able to overwhelm these objections by pointing to the much higher returns from tillage and to the successful experience of others pursuing a similar strategy in England, of which I had read in the various farming journals. I realised in due course, like many other silly young fools who choose to ignore the advice of their elders and betters, that the course I proposed to follow only looked better, and in reality was not. It looked better first, because I failed to perceive the many concealed obstacles in what I had decided on, and second, because those who urged caution poorly expressed their views, which reflected the wisdom of the ages: that life is difficult with many pitfalls, and that it is best to hold to tried and true ways and venture off these cautiously and experimentally. If this viewpoint is not always persuasive, it is not because it lacks truth but because those who hold to it are practical people, more accustomed to coping with life than to analysing life's problems and articulating ways of dealing with them.

Mortification at my callow disregard of the advice of elders and betters, for which of course an appropriately high price was duly paid, has subsequently been alleviated somewhat by observing other, older, more prestigious persons similarly flying in the face of established wisdom. I have frequently observed World Bank and similar so-called experts, who have never grown a crop or raised an animal in their lives, advising governments of Third World countries to embark on farm policies that conflicted with the local wisdom painfully acquired over the ages, with as much presumptuous arrogance as was my ploughing the entire good pastureland of the Dunbell farm in 1945.

My first year farming on my own account would have been my last year were it not for some good luck and for a tolerant bank manager. The summer and autumn of 1946, my first harvest year, were the wettest seasons on record, the next worst being 1846, which had washed out the potato crop and marked the depth of the Great Famine. It was the year before the introduction of selective weedkillers, which have since transformed cropgrowing in Ireland. The thistles, which flourish in all good grassland, flourished even better in the corn crops of the rain-drenched year of 1946. The little combine-harvester, probably one of the first dozen or so in Ireland, that I had bought on HP was totally inadequate for the situation. As a wag observed, "a milking machine" would have been more suitable than a combine harvester for harvesting the rain-soaked, thistle-infested harvest of 1946.

It seemed to rain or to snow continuously from July 1946 to March 1947. Then the weather changed and there was virtually no rain for nine months. The result over the eighteen months was the sort of average rainfall and sunshine statistics that give an utterly erroneous picture of the true weather conditions in nine years out of ten. Selective weedkillers meanwhile became available in 1947 and thistles in cereals ceased to be a problem. The dry season simplified all farm operations. 1947 was probably the most trouble-free year for tillage farming ever in Ireland. There was only one snag: it was also almost a crop free year. The land, drying quickly after months and months of continuous rain and snow, baked under a sun of an intensity more frequently encountered in the Mediterranean than in Ireland. Some fields yielded little more than their seed. Overall Irish cereal yields hit a new record low that year.

Again, only hope, good luck and tolerant creditors made it possible to embark on the third year farming. That, after the hurricanes of the first two years, was unremarkable. My position recovered sufficiently well to make possible what I now perceive to have been the wisest - perhaps the only wise - act of my life: marriage to the girl down the road, Biddy Kirwan.

By now most of my innocence had been dissipated - and I refer to economic rather than other brands of innocence. Easy money in large quantities was not readily available in Irish farming, and my freedom of action was much more circumscribed than formerly. The two initial bad years had got me heavily into debt to the bank, the local co-op and the HP company - though "heavily" here is relative. My total indebtedness at the worst period, before the third harvest, would have been no more than the small change of latter-day farmers whose debts, as they say, run into amounts "like telephone numbers". The option of a low cost-low output farming was no longer available. Servicing debt and maintaining what soon came to be a rapidly expanding family were overhead costs that could only be covered, if at all, from a large turnover.

Over the next few years I increased output per acre to around eight times the national average. This was possible through a mainly tillage programme which became technically more feasible during the 1950s. A new Massey-Harris combine harvester could cope with even the wettest harvest. One of the first combine corndrills in the country, which planted seed in a bed of fertilizer, made it possible to get much better returns from fertilizers than the old way of broadcasting these over the ground. Above all, selective weedkillers, which I had been one of the first to use on their introduction to Ireland in 1947, made it possible to depart with impunity from traditional, though constricting, good husbandry practices. It was possible with these and similar innovations to get high sustained yields on large acreages of sugarbeet, peas and grain.

These crop activities were supplemented with low capital intensity livestock enterprises. The first of these was poultry, when, like other misguided persons, I sought to implement Agriculture Minister Jim Dillon's threat "to drown England with eggs". When that particular bubble burst, I switched to pigs which, if they did not add much to net profit, did relieve cash-flow, as they nowadays say. The sale of the pigs yielded an income that was especially welcome in the pre-harvest months of "hungry" July and August, and the feed bills could be settled after the harvest. A lot of work and worry was involved, but without yielding the large income that in the days of my innocence I had foolishly expected. A fair living and some slow progress in getting the debt situation under control were about as much I achieved during the years 1948–1953.

This situation was as puzzling as it was unsatisfactory. It was the more puzzling in that the neighbouring farm was operated on principles as divergent from mine as was possible. The bachelor farmer who owned the farm was one of those made immortal by the ballad "The Bachelors of Dunbell". He "sowed not neither did he reap" but he seemed to do every bit as well, if not as Solomon, as I who did these things all day, all year long. A Hereford bull ran with his cow herd, which in due course produced calves which the cows suckled. The calves continued to suckle the cows until the following year's calf crop appeared. Then the cows, to reserve their milk for the new calf crop, drove off last year's calves which by then had developed sharp horns that must have made suckling unpleasant for the cows. The winter feed problem was dealt with principally by closing off several fields during the summer and letting the cattle in to graze them consecutively during the winter months. My neighbour also prepared for winter by selling off his surplus stock in the autumn. This was an interesting exercise.

Word went out that Roger was in the mood to sell. Cattle dealers who knew that there was profit in catering for his somewhat odd ways came to the farm, and with Roger's help rounded up the cattle. The cattle for sale were identified and a deal was easily struck at several pounds a head less than similar cattle would have been worth if sold under normal circumstances. Then the buyers had the job of sorting out and removing the purchased cattle. There the fun began.

Roger, unlike other farmers, never drove his stock. Instead he called them and they followed him wherever he wished to take them. When, however, the cattle dealers commenced to remove the cattle they had bought, pandemonium broke loose. I have since seen almost wild cattle on the African veld. I have watched South Americans on ponyback with their long, vicious whips drive cattle without mercy, stampeding them over the pampas. But neither I nor anyone else has ever witnessed mayhem like that which broke loose when the cattle buyers proceeded to remove the cattle they had bought from Roger's herd. The herd, which on every other day of the year was utterly docile and responded immediately to Roger's every command, seemed to summon up all the wildness of their auroch progenitors in a frenzy of bellowing, charging and general mayhem. But profit conquers all. If the return is sufficiently high people will do virtually anything, including buying and removing Roger's surplus cattle every autumn.

Apart from saving up a number of fields for winter grazing and removing all surplus stock in the autumn, Roger had another device for getting through the winter period of dearth without the hassle of hay or silage making. That was the age-old way of feeding the cattle beef-steaks, especially in the spring. Throughout the world cattle are held mainly in latitudes that are some distance from the equator. The higher latitudes, unlike equatorial regions, are characterized by pronounced seasonal variations, which may be wet and dry; or as in Ireland, cold in the winter and less cold in the summer. Only in European societies and in the societies of European origin in the New World do stockholders preserve surplus fodder made during the growing season for use in the dormant season. Elsewhere they do as my Dunbell neighbour Roger did: they let their cattle live off their stored-up fat during the later stages of the dormant period. Recent research suggests that Roger was not nearly as daft as I was inclined to regard him. It has now been established scientifically what Roger had figured out for himself: that the weight cattle lost from starvation in the spring, they quickly made good through a process referred to somewhat grandiloquently as "compensatory growth" during the summer months of abundance.

Of course not all the cattle survived the winters. The weaker ones perished and in doing so helped to produce a surviving strain of exceptionally hardy cattle able to live where others would not. But always there were cattle for sale in the autumn, even at a discount price. Income was small, but outgoings were zero. And when the one was deducted from the other Roger, who let his bull, cows and nature do the work and had an output per acre on good land less than half the national average, was not all that worse off than me, with an output per acre eight times the average.

If even the thickest skull survives long enough being knocked against a brick wall, a glimmer of light will seep through. I was not so busy growing beet, wheat, peas and so on that in the course of several years I could not give some thought to the point that Roger, who neither sowed nor reaped, appeared to be doing at least as well as I, who spent most of my time doing nothing else but sowing and reaping.

Stimulus was given to that as well as to other lines of thought by another factor. Paddy O'Keeffe, the dynamic young man who took over a faltering *Irish Farmers Journal* at the beginning of the 1950s and has since made it one of the most successful enterprises in the country and one of the most highly thought of farming papers in the world, had commissioned a weekly column from me under the *nom de plume* Tom Duffy. The need to fill that 500 word column forced upon me a degree of figuring and contemplation possibly above the norm for farmers or indeed for most of those engaged, as early censuses of occupation put it, in meeting "physical needs" as distinct from "moral needs". (The latter category embraced all shades of pen- and paper-pushers.)

Finally, of course, there was the need to salvage something of one's own *amour propre*. I had early on realized that, contrary to what, as an impressionable youth, I had gathered from the literature, making a packet from Irish farming involved more than applying a bag or two of superphosphate, measuring the milk output of the cows once a week, and feeding pigs on a less imbalanced diet than the emergency-time one of 100% broken brown bread. My overall output per acre was well above the national average. Crop yields, if not wildly exciting, were also above the average. Yet my total annual family farming income was no more than the £1000 which the Sugar Company costings showed I should be making on the 40 acres of sugarbeet grown. What about the other 160 acres of wheat, barley, peas and sheep?

After about seven years of farming on my own account, the idea began to dawn on me that in determining profits there is, besides output, another factor, inputs. Profits, or net income, were not determined as I had up to then implicitly accepted, by output; input was no less important. It seems incredible, but for the first seven years of my farming life I had proceeded on the principle that all one had to do was to produce. It says much for the security of tenure of Irish farmers in those days, after the landlords had been forced out and before the banks got their present stranglehold on the land, that I had not only managed to hold on in farming, but had made some modest progress in consolidating my position.

As consciousness dawned of the importance of the cost factor in the equation: Profit = Output-Costs, I also became aware of how those costs were raised in various ways. For example, every year Jimmy Lennon used to hire a plate for his lorry which allowed him to haul my beet and that of neighbouring farmers to Carlow Sugar Factory. The owner of the plate, who had acquired it in the same mysterious ways as others did when those plates were being allocated by government, contributed nothing other than the use of the plate to the production of the sugarbeet, yet he seemed to make more out of the beet than I or any of those who shared in the hard graft of growing the stuff, from muck-spreading to loading the beet on to a lorry.

This was an interesting line of enquiry. To take the case of fertilizers, of which I used large quantities, Irish manufacturers were protected, so fertilizers cost more than they would if there was free trade. The same held true for ploughs, shovels, forks, hoes, etc., etc. One could even say that the wages I paid were higher than they would otherwise have been because workers had to pay more for their boots, clothes and so on which they were forced to buy from protected Irish producers.

It was of course not entirely a one-sided business. The boot and clothes makers had to pay more for bread and sugar because these were made from home-grown raw materials for which I and other farmers got higher than world prices. But because the vastly greater proportion of Irish farmland produced cattle, which were exported at world prices, the price of other farm commodities produced exclusively for the home market, particularly wheat and sugarbeet, could not diverge very greatly from world levels. Otherwise farmers producing cattle for sale at world prices would divert more land to producing wheat and sugarbeet and flood the small local market with these. The degree of effective protection given to non-agricultural industry was a lot higher than that given to agriculture.

The rights and wrongs of protecting industry or of having cost-raising controls on road transport were not of interest to me. Presumably there were good reasons for these policies. But more and more clearly I came to see that the manner of implementing the policies was wrong. Government in its wisdom had policies; it was the obligation of citizens, including farmers, to pay for these. But surely a farmer's obligation to pay for national policies should be proportionate to the amount of land he/she held rather than the use made of that land?

Payment of the farmer's share of the cost of national policies according to the amount of land held, rather than the use made of it, seemed right on grounds of equity as well as economic expedience. The person with 100 acres of land would seem in all reason to have a greater obligation to society than the person with 50 acres. That, for example, was the case in establishing the individual's contribution to the upkeep of the Church: the "dues" were pitched according to the value of the parishioner's property. It was also the case with various farmer organisations, membership fees for which were usually based on the number of acres farmed.

It seemed economically expedient that the cost of government policy should be levied on farmers according to the amount of land they held rather than the use they made of it. After all, expanding agricultural output had been a main plank of all Irish governments from the time of the state's first Minister for Agriculture, Paddy Hogan. He it was who popularised the rhyme (which, however, remained more aspiration than realisation):

> one more cow, one more sow,
> one more acre under the plough.

Indeed that objective predated the state, increased agricultural output having been the concern of the Irish Department of Agriculture, which was one of the oldest in the world, dating back to 1899. Apart from its venerable institutional age, the

Irish Department of Agriculture was also one of the most costly of such establishments relative to Gross National Product. It was axiomatic that the country wanted greater agricultural output. Yet levying the cost of policy on farmers according to the use they made of the land rather than according to the amount of land they held was the surest possible way of depressing output. It forced up the cost of everything the farmer needed for production. And, as in the case of the lorry plate which Jimmy Lennon had to hire, it reduced the ex-farm value of everything that was produced.

Ever so slowly these elementary concepts evolved in my little brain. Clarification was greatly expedited by Sean Moylan, whom I never met but who was nonetheless one of the principal formative influences in my life. Sean Moylan of Mallow, who had been Minister for Agriculture in a Fianna Fail government but was then Opposition spokesman on agriculture, wrote commending one of my "Tom Duffy" articles in the Irish Farmers' Journal. The article dealt with Jim Dillon's Land Rehabilitation Scheme "to push the rocks of Connemara into the Atlantic Ocean", as he put it in a typically flamboyant piece of Dillonesque.

Because Jim Dillon was in hurry to make an impact with his Land Rehabilitation Scheme and because farmers, with memories of the Economic War of the 1930s still fairly fresh, were hesitant to avail of it, the Department of Agriculture set up its own teams of contractors, equipped with the latest, most massive and most expensive bulldozers and other earth-moving equipment. One of these teams, owned by the Department of Agriculture, undertook a very large rehabilitation exercise on a farm of some 1000 acres bounding mine. That farm had been put together by a returned Australian who reportedly had got rich hijacking the diamonds of other miners rather than digging his own. He used his wealth to "grab" the land of evicted tenant farmers during the Land War, by paying their arrears of rent. In this way, several family farms had been amalgamated to create a "ranch". The "grabbed" land had been farmed on ranch principles, that is, with minimal inputs over a period of 60 - 70 years. By then much of the land had reverted to nature as bushes, thorns and poor trees took over. This land was now being rehabilitated with equipment owned by the Irish state, at great cost to Irish taxpayers but virtually free for the landowner.

Two aspects of the exercise appeared to be particularly ironic. I watched on one occasion a huge bulldozer owned by the Department clearing the remnants of a farm-dwelling: the chimney stack, the hearthstone and the foundations of the walls. Returning emigrants would look in vain for a trace of the dwelling in which their forebears had lived and from which they had been evicted.

My own farm being on elevated land, or a Carn, offered a good prospect over the surrounding territory. As the rehabilitation of the 1000 acres proceeded, there were numerous fires to burn the scrub and trees bulldozed from the neglected land. These fires were always well soused with diesel oil for a good reason, other than to promote combustion. As I said, the creation and management of these teams of contractors by the Department of Agriculture was to satisfy Jim Dillon's urge to get his Land Rehabilitation Scheme into operation as quickly and widely as possible. It was precisely the sort of activity in which no branch of government should ever engage. Control required methods and resources altogether alien to a bureaucracy. One of the hastily devised control measures for these teams was the amount of diesel fuel consumed. If a lot of fuel was used, a lot of work was assumed to have been done and questions were not asked. It was in everyone's interest (apart from the taxpayer's) to use copious amounts of diesel fuel to ignite and burn the thresh that was the product of decades of neglect of a thousand acres of land grabbed from evicted tenants.

It was an article by me in the *Irish Farmers Journal* critical of these matters that evoked the response from Sean Moylan. That letter gave rise to a desultory correspondence between us, no more than a couple of letters each way over as many years. This slight contact with a person who was clearly of exceptional ability and exceptionally concerned with the public good was my licence to seek his help on the problem with which I was wrangling more and more: why shouldn't farmers' share of the cost of implementing public policy be based on the amount of land held rather than on the use made of that land?

There was a long, sympathetic and informative reply from Sean Moylan, bless him. As well as helping to clarify and set right some aspects of my ideas, the letter pointed out that these were not quite as novel as I thought they were. What I was advocating essentially was a tax on land in place of other impositions. Subsequently I learned that people have been as regularly and frequently discovering the merits of taxing land as others have been discovering the wheel! Sean Moylan suggested that I read Henry George's *Progress and Poverty*, published in the USA in 1880. The impression that made on me recalls Keats's sonnet, "On First Looking into Chapman's Homer":

> Then felt I like some watcher of the skies,
> When a new planet swims into his ken;
> Or like stout Cortez when, with eagle eyes,
> He gazed at the Pacific, and all his men
> Looked at each other with a wild surmise
> Silent, upon a peak in Darien.

All the bits and pieces with which I had struggled so painfully and ponderously seemed now to fall so easily and neatly into place. Though man might be, as Aristotle observed, a rational animal, he does not always behave as one, especially in the manner in which he organizes his relations with his fellow men. Every consideration of efficiency and equity pointed to taxing land rather than what went into, or came from, land. Yet in Ireland especially, virtually everything but land was taxed.

An intellect that had lain dormant at least for the years since leaving St. Kieran's College was brought back into unaccustomed use and stretched, as I went on from reading George to study the classical economists and political scientists, in inexpensive Everyman editions sold by Fred Hanna of Nassau Street, Dublin. Hobbes's *Leviathan,* Locke's *Treatise on Civil Government,* Hume's *Treatise of Human Nature*, Rousseau's *Social Contract,* Adam Smith's *Wealth of Nations,* Ricardo's *Principles of Political Economy and Taxation,* Malthus's *Essay on the Principles of Population;* and so on, up to John Stuart Mill. Inevitably I came to read Marx and his disciples in low cost, good quality editions from the New Bookshop in Parliament Street, Dublin.

This was like water in the intellectual aridity of Irish farming. But as floods of water on parched land can often be destabilising, so this flood of ideas becoming suddenly available to one whose formal education had not proceeded beyond matriculation, at that time little more than a formality, left me in the end as bewildered and uncomprehending as at the commencement. Smith, Marx, Rousseau, Mills, or whichever I had last read appeared to have incontrovertible supporting arguments, so that by times I was a Georgist, a Marxist, a Malthusianist, and so on.

I did, however, have the wit to realize that this quite undisciplined and undirected study was not helping me much in what I now perceived to be life's principal task: "rerum cognoscere causas", or "of things to understand the causes". Specifically, I wanted to understand why making a pile out of Irish farming was by no means as easy as I had thought it to be and as many in high places still seemed to think it was. I wanted to understand further why government, while saying it wanted agricultural output to expand, pursued policies that were directly contrary to that objective. For, if I read the situation correctly, the way to make money from Irish farming was to produce, not much, as I had been doing and as governments advocated, but little.

It had taken me almost ten years of farming on my own account to learn this basic truth of Irish farming: it's not how much you get out, it's how little you put in that determines financial success or failure in Irish farming. Apart from natural obtuseness, my town-rearing had been responsible for my taking so long to learn this elementary truth which every person growing up on an Irish farm absorbs as naturally as mother's milk. Objective reasoning from the facts said this. Prices were lower and/or costs were higher in Ireland. Therefore, it was economically sensible not to use much of the higher cost inputs to produce much of the lower priced outputs. The secret was to see how little one could get away with spending and to let the output take care of itself.

The successful people in Irish farming were those who innovated little; who held their operating costs to a minimum; and who when they sought to expand did so laterally rather than perpendicularly. That is to say, if they had spare resources to invest, they invested them in acquiring more land rather than in producing more from the land already held. Acquiring additional land to operate on a low-cost/low-output basis made sense given that the cost of holding that land was virtually zero. The cost of holding land was the nominal charge of the local government rates or taxes. Because these were based on the utterly out-of-date Griffin valuation of the 1840s, the Supreme Court has since found them to be unconstitutional; and the position at time of writing (1987) is that there are now no taxes whatever on Irish land. If in time the land reverts to scrub from neglect, there is always the likelihood that some EEC equivalent of Jim Dillon's Land Rehabilitation Scheme will come along to rehabilitate it gratis. The basic rule of successful Irish farming was almost as simple as: keep off the grass; let nature grow the stuff; and allow the cattle to fatten on it.

I had no stomach for that sort of cautious, Spartan farming. A life in which one's principal piece of equipment was a stout belt for fastening was a poor enough prospect, and as different as conceivable from my approach to farming in 1942 when I first left school. It was a much more realistic one, but realism was not the touchstone. I realized that in my imprudent, reckless way, I had stumbled upon a truth of great importance that I could not just let lie there:

And that one talent which is death to hide,
Lodged with me useless though my soul more bent
To serve therewith my Maker and present
My true account lest he returning chide.

It was accepted as axiomatic that the wellbeing, the very existence of the Irish nation depended closely on the productive use of the nation's land. That would provide the raw materials for industrial processing and the exports to pay for essential imports of raw material and capital goods. The posture of successive governments was to encourage and facilitate agricultural expansion. The main instrument of expansion was the Department of Agriculture which, as already noted, is one of the oldest in the world and at that time was perhaps the most expensive relative to Gross National Product. But that was mere posturing. While agricultural advisors, paid for ultimately by the state, urged farmers to use more fertilizers, for example, the government's fiscal policy of taxing everything bar land including, directly or indirectly, fertilizers, made it unprofitable to use those fertilizers. Government policy instead made it profitable to retain land underfertilized and "producing as little as was possible to produce under an Irish sky", as a New Zealand expert engaged by James Dillon described the situation.

To develop and express this insight appeared to be supremely important. But how to do so was not immediately obvious. I was devouring the classics of political economics but was floundering in the mass of new and exciting knowledge. I was failing to marshal that knowledge; and I was failing to use it first to specify clearly the problem I had stumbled upon, and second to identify ways in which to resolve it.

A university course, such as I had spurned on leaving St. Kieran's, was indicated. That, I hoped, would help to put order on the mass of wild and turbulent ideas which study of the politico- economic classics had created. But in 1955, at 30 years of age, married with "a biological" family of five children, an overdraft, and living 70 miles from Dublin, a university education seemed fanciful, even to me.

I put the problem to my friend and former mentor, Frank Hussey, at the Albert Agricultural College. I could not have consulted a better person. He, quite unknown to me, had taken, after an NUI degree in Agriculture, a London University external degree in Economics. He suggested that such a degree might be appropriate to my circumstances. It was indeed.

By the end of 1955, I had established that to study as an external student for a B.Sc.(Econ.) degree at the University of London, I would have to pass the English General Certificate of Education at advanced, or A, level in three subjects. The course itself could be taken completely by correspondence through a subsidiary of the University, the Commerce Degree Bureau. It could be completed at that time in a minimum of three years, though normally in five years, which has since been made also the minimum period of study. These facilities seemed ideal.

I thoroughly reorganized the farm in line with my newly found economic wisdom. This involved firing five of the six men I had previously employed and selling two of the three tractors and a great deal of the equipment. I bought 60 in-calf Kerry heifers in Killarney at an average price of £18 each and built what was one of the first yard/milking shed arrangements in Ireland.

Aoibhinn Beatha an Scoileareacht

I settled down to study at the beginning of 1956, first for the required GEC (A) level passes and subsequently for the B.Sc.(Econ). (Beyond that it was my intention to write a book to explain why Irish farming was not making the contribution that it should to national wellbeing and to identify the measures necessary to cause it to do so. This came to pass with the publication in 1966 by Cork University Press of my *Irish Agricultural Production; Its Volume and Structure.*) The transformation was achieved with incredible ease. This was especially so by contrast with the hassle, the continuous under-performance and the endless disappointments of the preceding ten years of intensive, enthusiastic, but utterly misconceived farming. It took some little time for my wife and the remaining farm worker, Mickey Ryan, to realise that I was available to discuss and take decisions on the day-to-day problems that arise even in the most simplified farming systems only at breakfast time, dinner time and supper time. In between they would have to cope as best they could; which, of course, they did excellently.

I did an about-turn in farming policy. Instead of attempting to maximize output, I systematically set about minimizing inputs. Production was reduced to three products: grain, milk and calves. The latter were after a white, beef-type Shorthorn bull, which cost little. It was inexpensive because white bulls were generally unpopular; but on Kerry cows they can produce remarkably good-looking calves which, to the uninitiated, could easily pass as Aberdeen Angus crosses. The calf-purchasers of course knew their parent stock, yet returned spring after spring to haggle with Biddy, my wife, for hours on the doorstep over the calf price. The calves produced an income in early spring; the milk during the summer months; and the grain in the autumn. Milk yields, of course, were only a mere fraction of what is normal now; and the price was only 1/6d (about eight new pence) a gallon compared to 80p now. So the revenue was not much more than a twentieth of what a 55 cow herd would yield now; but operating costs were proportionately even less. The cows grazed on lightly manured short leas, which restored the land sufficiently for cereal cash crops. During the winter the hardy Kerry cows, bless 'em, survived well enough on barley straw ad lib and stubble grazing, supplemented with a very little hay. Even then, in the course of a few years they developed into animals which, apart from their black colour, were scarcely distinguishable from Shorthorns.

I studied from 7.00 am to 11.00 pm with some breaks. The first was for breakfast, when I discussed with Mickey the day's farming operations. The next was for dinner when I also took a walk around the farm to keep apprised. The final break was for an evening meal. The day finished at 11.00 pm when I went for a stroll in the deserted country lanes before turning in.

There were other breaks in this otherwise rigidly adhered routine. On Wednesday evenings Biddy and I went for a couple of drinks at the boozer. At weekends I took over from Mickey to milk the cows and deliver the milk to the local creamery. At harvest time also it was necessary to help on the combine-harvester. And each summer I took a week off "to do" in sequence the "Three Sisters" rivers, the Nore, the Suir and the Barrow.

I had come to perceive cruising down an Irish river as the epitome of relaxation, carried along mainly by the current and only slightly by paddling. So each summer during that period of study, in a canoe built to a standard design and fabricated of plywood and light canvas in the days before the extensive use of fibreglass, I set off from close to the headwaters of one or other of the Three Sisters. Equipped with tent, Primus stove and food replenished at the villages through which the river flowed, I allowed the current principally to carry me to the river's mouth. As the opportunity and mood suggested, I spent the night in the tent on the river's bank; or in a nearby hotel if one happened. One rarely saw or met a soul except when passing through villages. If there were other canoes in

Ireland then, they had not reached the Three Sisters.

In 1956 I travelled my own Nore from Freshford to New Ross, going as the current determined; negotiating with no great difficulty the various shallows and weirs en route. Next year it was the Barrow from above Portarlington, this time around Cheek Point, the confluence of the Three Sisters, and up the Suir to Waterford. In 1958 it was the turn for the Suir, starting on a tributary at Drish Bridge near Thurles and again ending in Waterford. That year was the wettest since my first farming year 1946, but the bad weather, which lodged the barley before the end of May in 1958, was little more than an inconvenience. I was growing much less corn and, although lodged, the crops were clean, having been sprayed with selective weedkillers. With a Massy-Harris combine-harvester it was possible to snatch and save even the worst lodged crops in the odd hour of dryness that occurs even in the wettest season.

The summer in which I took my degree, 1959, was as glorious as the preceding one had been wretched. That summer I spent messing around on the river Nore with the family, which by then had increased to seven in number, plus Biddy and me.

The four years during which I studied, 1956-59, when I spent no more than two hours a day on average on the farm and when production was less than a quarter of its previous peak level, were far and away my most successful farming years. They were virtually free of financial worry. At the same time as I was working towards a good academic qualification, I was beginning to get the debt position under control. If I had needed any other evidence, the experience of those years clinched the correctness of my analysis of the economics of Irish agriculture.

The studies proceeded as satisfyingly and trouble-free as the farming. That was due principally to two most wonderful institutions: the Commerce Degree Bureau of London University and the Irish Central Library for Students.

The Commerce Degree Bureau was established under the aegis of London University to give correspondence courses for students taking external degrees. For very modest fees, students had the services of the University's teaching staff

22

who designed course study notes, prepared reading lists, and commented in great detail and most beneficially on the many essays written while taking the course. Thousands of students from all over the world have benefited from using the Commerce Degree Bureau's services. They are all likely, like me, to have an abiding sense of gratitude to an institution which serves so well people from other lands who have no possible financial, political or other claim on London University or its subsidiary Commerce Degree Bureau.

The Irish Central Library for Students was, in my view, Ireland's finest institution. Of the hundreds of requests for books and journals that I made to it between 1956 and 1959, it did not fail to meet a single one. If the book or journal was unavailable from its own stocks, it borrowed from cooperating Irish libraries. If these did not have it, the request went to the British Library which sought for the required work amongst its own vast stocks; and if these failed, from among all the cooperating academic and public libraries in Britain.

I recall one item: a recent edition of the collected works of Machiavelli with an introduction by a Jesuit scholar. The introduction was part of the recommended reading on *The Prince*. As a result of scouring the whole Irish and British cooperating library system, the Irish Central Library for Students was able to offer a dozen or more different editions of the collected works of Machiavelli. But none of these had the required introduction and so did not meet my requirements. To meet these the Central Library bought the required edition at considerable expense, even in those days, and duly supplied it to me.

Daily, Dick Barmbrick, our postman, pushed his bicycle up the hill to the farmhouse to deposit a parcel of books, big or small. Only later when I went to read in the library at the London School of Economics did I appreciate how well I was served by the Irish Central Library for Students and Dick Barmbrick. Thanks to both of them I had every book and article I wanted, scoured if necessary from the combined Irish and British library services, delivered literally to my doorstep when I wanted them and pretty well for as long as I wanted. I could then read the works in the leisure and comfort of my own sitting-room. By contrast, LSE undergraduate students, using the old British Library of Political and Economic Science, had to squat on stairs or passageways, wherever they could find a spot to read the works that they, and probably a few dozen other students, had simultaneously requisitioned from the library staff. Only with difficulty and on a very restricted basis could they take some of these books to their homes or lodgings to study there.

Those four years of studying were without question the most satisfying of my life. Every day there was something to be learned that was new and relevant; that answered some outstanding question or raised some new one. In my early thirties, my brain was still sufficiently supple to grasp fairly readily new concepts, and my experience of the real world was already sufficiently extensive to have raised a host of questions in my mind which the readings merely served to answer. Much of the teacher's work when dealing with less mature students is in provoking curiosity – pointing out some remarkable phenomenon in nature, history or social affairs and encouraging students to wonder about it and to seek an explanation for it. The remainder of the work is suggesting an appropriate explanation. All, or most, of the questions were already there in my case. I had quit active farming, where the questions had been raised, and turned to study in order to seek an answer to the questions.

The answers flowed in as profusely as the books Dick Barmbrick delivered, profusely and possibly also somewhat facilely. In retrospect, the whole experience was rather akin to tropical plant growth. There was a flood of formal learning into an Irish farming situation that was intellectually arid, though no more so than any other farming situation that I have since observed in any other former colony of the capitalist system.

The result of this mountain of learning was a very modest mouse of academic achievement. I got a second class honours with only a couple of mildly distinctive features. First I got it in the minimum permitted time, which was then three years but has since been extended to five. And second, I was I believe the first external student of London University to take Mathematical Economics as an optional subject in the final

Part II degree examination.

Armed with a reasonable London University degree, owner of a good farm that was making money now that I realised that the key to success in Irish farming was to minimize inputs, the ball, so to speak was at my feet. The sensible thing to have done would have been to continue the very simple but profitable and reliable farming system I had evolved, while taking an off-farm job to absorb the time and energy I had been expending in studying.

Ireland in 1959 was embarking on the period of "economic miracles" of which Garret FitzGerald was then wont to write and which flowed from the policies that were heralded by *Economic Development*. That document, which had been published by the government in the preceding year, had been authored by the Secretary of the Department of Finance and head of the Civil Service, T.K. Whitaker, himself the holder of a London external B.Sc.(Econ) degree. There was a perceived need for economists in government and other employments; and there were not very many available. There was, so far as I knew, none who combined a good training in economics with the sort of practical experience I had had in Irish farming. A range of job choices was available. Jf personal advancement was the concern, then the way ahead was very clear in 1959. It was to continue farming on the established lines; to hold down a good job during the week; relieve the man on the farm at weekends; clear the outstanding overdraft; and buy more land as it came on the market. But it was never a seriously considered proposition.

Four years of systematic study and two preceding years of unsystematic devouring of the political-economic classics had left me more convinced than ever of both the correctness and the importance of the insight upon which I had stumbled. This was that it was both inequitable and inexpedient to make farmers pay their share of the cost of implementing government policy according to the use that they made of the land which they held. Farmers instead should be required to pay according to the amount of that land that they held.

The sort of economic crisis which had occurred in Ireland in 1956, and which was itself only a worsening of conditions that at all times were unsatisfactory, was inevitable given the existing situation. How could there be economic progress if agriculture continued to stagnate? My own experience and everything I had learned about economics showed that Irish farming was bound to stagnate as long as the cost of government policy was levied on what farmers bought and sold rather than on the land they held. Any farmer crazy enough to buck that trend would meet only trouble, as I had discovered to my cost.

Given these circumstances, the ballyhoo that was then current about T.K. Whitaker's *Economic Development* was clearly nothing more than ballyhoo. It was merely a new twist to old, fatally flawed policies.The first Coalition government, under J.A. Costello, had discovered the delights of Keynesian economics at a time when it was said "we are all Keynesians now". Keynes had pointed to the lack of demand as a factor in creating unemployment in Britain and showed that, contrary to the established orthodoxy, there was no automatic mechanism to ensure that demand would be at a level to ensure full employment. He went on to argue that it was the responsibility of government to raise an inadequate demand up to a full employment level by spending more than it took out of the economy through taxation; or by public sector deficit financing, in today's jargon.

The gravest, most complex and subtle doubts have since been raised about this proposition which, however, in 1948 was a concept on the frontiers of knowledge of economics. It was therefore intellectually respectable and politically advantageous for the Coalition government to do what no Irish administration had done since the old Irish Parliament. That Parliament had been forced to legislate itself out of existence by the Act of Union of 1800, largely because it had become hopelessly indebted and dependent on the London government to bail it out. But that experience had been forgotten and Irish governments were once more prepared to embark systematically on a programme of borrowing. "If", the politicians argued, "it was in order for the USA and Great Britain to borrow massively to fight an enormously destructive war, it had to be sensible for Ireland to borrow for national development."

The proposition was irrefutable. Keynes had cut the

intellectual ground from under the exponents of the traditional "dreary science" of economics. As people like Professor Patrick Lynch, then reaching the apex of his abilities and influence, pointed out to the timorous: "internal borrowing involved internal transfers only and so did not affect the main macro-economic variables." Persons with funds to lend jumped at the opportunity of lending to the government at 3% instead of getting a miserable 1% on bank deposits. And of course those who got jobs and incomes from the increased expenditure were also enthusiastic. This last group included, after a time when its merits sank through, those farmers who belatedly availed of Jim Dillon's Land Reclamation Scheme.

The Coalition initiators of public sector deficit financing got two terms of office out of this radical departure from the stern fiscal rectitude that had characterised all Irish administrations since the Act of Union. The Coalition's first term had been brought to an untimely end by the falling out over Dr. Noel Browne's Mother and Child Scheme. Its second term was ended abruptly by the acute balance of payments problem caused by the government spending more than it took in taxation.

As government spent money on houses, schools and hospitals, the workers and others who received the money spent a good deal of it on imported goods. Virtually all of the money used by government to buy bulldozers to clear the scrub from the neglected, grabbed land of ranchers and to buy diesel oil to burn the cleared scrub, went directly out of the country. None of these activities generated additional exports, and that included Jim Dillon's Land Reclamation Scheme, which failed like everything else to raise agricultural output. With imports increasing while exports remained unaffected by government deficit financing, substantial balance of payments deficits inevitably arose. The sterling assets, which had been built up during the war years when there was nothing available to buy with the money Britain paid for Irish agricultural exports, were dissipated within a few years. The precious monetary reserves, which guarantee the convertibility into English pounds of the pounds issued by the Irish Central Bank, were disappearing like snuff at a wake.

The government, in order to halt the outflow, apparently had no option but to cut spending. This precipitated the great economic crisis of the 1950s, when the number at work fell from 1,250,000 in 1955 to 1,050,000 in 1958, at which level, after a temporary increase of some 100,000 in the 1970s, it has remained up to now. Emigration during those years, when I was ensconced in my study working for the B.Sc.(Econ.) and farming profitably, was at a higher rate than at any time since the 1870s. During the worst years as many people emigrated from Ireland as were born there, causing a serious decline in population.

Whitaker's *Economic Development,* appearing in 1958 at the bottom of the slump, heralded a change in economic policy. The change was one of emphasis rather than substance; but it had medium-term beneficial effects which reinforced the natural recovery from the trough of the slump. The much trumpeted publication advocated, and was followed by, a shift in emphasis of government expenditure from houses, hospitals and schools which, as noted, increased imports and not exports, to factories, offices and hotels. The latter did increase exports. This pattern of expenditure also encouraged investment by foreigners in Ireland to avail of the grants and tax holidays which the Irish government was now offering to those producing for export. The government paid for the grants and tax holidays from borrowed funds.

Whitakerism, by countering the immediate balance of payments deficit that followed from the first exercise of sustained deficit financing by an Irish government since the eighteenth century, gave a new and much longer lease of life to the practice. Provided government has credit – and a century-and-a-half of strict financial rectitude, pursued regardless of its social costs, had earned for the Irish state an almost unparalleled credit rating – virtually anything is possible. In this case it was very easy for the state, using borrowed funds, to subsidise the establishment of enclave exporting industries and to exempt these from taxes on their accounting profits. There was an immediate stimulus to exports and in so far as earnings from these did not pay for all imports, the gap was more than made good by foreigners investing in the new factories that the Whitaker departure made profitable in Ireland.

There was, as I pointed out in my *Irish Agricultural Production* (1966), an impossible defect in what was essentially merely an expedient to prolong the stimulation of the economy by public sector deficit financing. This was that as the public debt increased from its 1958 proportions, the cost to taxpayers of servicing it would also increase. That in turn would raise costs for Irish agriculture and manufacturing industry and make production in these, in so far as it was not subsidised by deficit financed government subsidies, even less rewarding than it already was. This would call for still further government subsidies and still more state borrowing, which must sooner or later spill over into external borrowing and culminate in the morass of domestic and foreign debt in which the Irish economy is now utterly stranded.

The prognosis was perfectly clear to me in 1959. That was partly because of the formal understanding of economics which I had acquired in reading for the London degree course, but mainly because I was now fully alert to the utterly wrong policies that were being pursued in relation to agriculture. There was nothing in Whitaker's *Economic Development* to give the slightest expectation that matters would be different in future. Without a more efficient mobilization of the nation's very considerable agricultural resources, there was no prospect of progress. Whatever temporary benefits were secured by the Whitaker expedient would of their nature be transient and would leave the economy weaker and poorer in the long run. It seemed clear that if government could not cope with the old but elementary problem of making Irish agriculture a little less inefficient, it was poppycock to think it could cope any better with the new task it was setting itself, to launch the country into sustained, competitive manufacturing for export.

It was therefore more clear than ever in 1959 that this country of mine was in dire trouble and was being set on a course that was bound to immerse it deeper and deeper. The knowledge and insights which I had gained from farming and from studying I was convinced offered the country the possibility of a radically different course which could save it from the disasters that lay in the course that was now being

29

pursued.

There was never any question of pursuing the attractive possibilities for personal advancement which, in 1959, the combination of a simple, foolproof, profitable farming system and a University of London degree in Economics offered. It appeared to me that it profits a man nothing if he gains the whole world while in the process the society of which he is a member dissolves in chaos. There was no assurance that it would be possible to ward off the chaos, but there was a clear duty to do what one could. Thirty years ago the prospects of being able to do something effective towards warding off the approaching disaster seemed brighter than they do now.

The course ahead was clear, to develop and express those insights into the economics of Irish agriculture which experience and study had furnished me; and to present these as clearly and as persuasively as possible to the Irish public. The first step in doing this was to learn the techniques of social science research, by taking a postgraduate qualification; and then to write and publish a work on the economics of Irish agriculture.

My first degree gained me access to the Graduate School of the London School of Economics, a constituent college of London University. I studied there from 1959 to 1961 for the M.Sc. (Econ) degree. In 1961 I went to University College Wales, Aberystwyth, to lecture in Agricultural Economics, and while there wrote *Irish Agricultural Production; Its Volume and Structure* which was published by Cork University Press in 1966.

CHAPTER 2

The Development of Undevelopment

Who Only Ireland Knows

The Irish establishment, more durable than the walls of Jericho, did not crumble when *Irish Agricultural Production* was published. Indeed, apart from the odd, mainly favourable notice in obscure journals, Ireland and the world proceeded after the book's publication precisely as they had done before. Academic argument, however cogent, impinges little, if at all, on the course of events.

The broad outline and general thrust of the book had occurred to me while still farming full blast in Dunbell, Kilkenny. The essence of my thought was that the land of Ireland belongs to the people of Ireland, equally to the entire people of Ireland. Property in Irish land had been a disaster for the nation ever since its creation by the confiscation of the clans' lands under the Tudor monarchs; and it continued to be so. Unless the Conquest could be undone by causing Irish land to be used efficiently and once more for the benefit of all the people, the Irish economy could not prosper.

The necessary and sufficient condition for having Irish land operated efficiently on behalf of all the people is that it should be taxed to its full annual value. Land's full annual value is broadly equivalent to the "rack rents" that Anglo-Irish landlords extracted in the 19th century; or the competitive rents that Irish farmers extract for the one-tenth of all land that continues to be let out on yearly tenancies. The revenue from a tax on land would make it possible to reduce, or to remove, taxes on the inputs to and the outputs from land.

A land tax would ensure that only those best able to

operate the land would continue to do so. The others would retire or take up other jobs; or, probably most frequently, give up all but the land that they could operate efficiently. There would be no need for a Department of Agriculture, for the proposed land tax would, far more effectively than that institution, secure the efficient use of the nation's land. The savings from closing down this costly Department would make possible further reductions in taxes on the inputs to, and the outputs from, land.

The combination of a tax on land and the removal of taxes on inputs to, and outputs from, land would transform Irish agriculture. It could easily cause it to double output virtually overnight. This large and rapid expansion in output would arise because the land tax would replace what are arguably the least efficient farmers in the world by persons who would be likely to be among the most efficient. Expansion would also occur because, as a result of the reduction in the cost of inputs and an increase in the value of outputs, efficient farmers would use many more non-land inputs to produce greater outputs.

When I removed with my family first to London and then to Aberystwyth, the farm at Dunbell had been let on conacre, or on a succession of one-year tenancies, during the seven years. As soon as *Irish Agricultural Production,* with its central proposal to tax away the annual value of land, was published, I offered the farm to the Irish Land Commission, because by then property in land had become obnoxious to me.

Property takes different forms. Property in things which people produce but do not consume, or capital, has been the key to man's realization of his vast potential as a rational being, without which he could never have raised far above the brute beast. But property in land I now perceived to be hardly less socially inequitable than property in man, or slavery, which Aristotle described as "the first, the best and most useful form of property". Indeed, some might deem property in land to be more heinously anti-social. One recalls, for example, that while a million Irish people starved to death during the 1840s so as to maintain or increase the profit from Irish land, the negro slaves of the United States of America, without any augmentation from the slave trade which by then had been stopped, were increasing in numbers by 2.5% annually. This was possibly the highest rate of natural population growth in the world at the time. Indubitably many starving, rack-rented Irish peasants, if given the choice, would have opted for slavery rather than to be the victims of property in Irish land.

I would have escaped sooner from the burden of land ownership but to have done so would have exposed me to the charge of first selling land and then proposing to tax its value away. Offering it to the Land Commission at their valuation, following publication of my book, appeared to be the least culpable way of disposing of a disagreeable responsibility. It would of course have been possible and profitable to have retained the land and to have continued to draw the conacre rent. Unless Irish economic history was to be turned on its head, that rent could have been relied upon to increase over time at least as rapidly as the cost of living. The spoils of the system could in that way have been used to sustain such efforts as I could make to end a system which appeared to be utterly incompatible with the social wellbeing. There were good precedents for that sort of approach: the illustrious Frederick Engels used the profits of his textile mills to sustain himself and Marx in their onslaught on the capitalist system which generated those profits. For my part, I was unsure of being able to sustain a committed attack on property in Irish land if I continued to profit from that institution. Moreover, even the minimum effort required to manage land being let on conacre had become impossibly tiresome, distracting my modest capacities from the more important task of understanding why the economy failed to serve adequately the Irish people.

Ireland in 1966 was experiencing its age of "economic miracles", as Garret FitzGerald was given to describing the recovery from the depression of 1958. The last thing Ireland was interested in just then was the sort of radical reform necessary to rectify the underlying structural defects in its economy. These latter would only surface again, in magnified form, when the state's credit was exhausted and it was no longer possible to pay with borrowed funds the subsidies that financed the Irish "economic miracle ".

There was no question of being able to return to Ireland to

participate in implementing radical reform. Nor was I willing to reintegrate back into the Irish economy, holding there whatever appointment was available and serving a socio-economic order that was inequitable and inefficient in the extreme and was bound to fail sooner rather than later. It would have been perfectly possible to continue as a lecturer in Agricultural Economics at the University of Wales. Life was pleasant in Aberystwyth; it was a very civilized existence, and our children were doing well at school. With a publication of some substance to my name within five years of appointment, there was the expectation of at least normal advancement in an academic career. The snag was that I was not cut out to be an academic. It was time to move on.

The "development industry" was in the full flush of its early growth in 1966. The world's consciousness had been awakened to the problems of poverty in the countries of Asia, Africa and the Caribbean, which had recently become independent or were in the process of gaining their independence, as well as to those of Latin America which had been independent for much longer. Following a score of years of rapid economic recovery from the destruction of the Second World War and of sustained economic growth under the influence of Keynesian type policies, the western world had the resources to expend in what has since come to be known as the Third World. The West, too, had confidence that by the judicious use of those resources its own rapid economic growth could be repeated elsewhere, so raising the Third World to a higher plane of existence. My unusual combination of farming experience and academic training made it easy to find employment that was not uncomfortable and was reasonably remunerative in this relatively new "development industry". From a home in Kilkenny where it was possible to maintain contact with Irish affairs, I worked as an economic advisor for various agencies in a score of Third World countries in South East Asia, South Asia, Africa, the Caribbean and South America, over the following nine years.

I was fortunate in being able to find a particular niche among the ranks of economic advisors to the Third World. These, even twenty years ago, were numerous and were being added to daily, frequently by people of outstanding ability.

Few of these, even those who specialised in agricultural economics, had practical experience of farming, which of course is of overwhelming importance in all Third World countries. That want of practical experience did not preclude study, analysis and recommendation on the cropgrowing component, which often is the most important in Third World farming. But few advisors dabbled in livestock matters, partly because these appeared to be relatively unimportant, but mainly because even to the brashest the topic was *terra incognita*, lying beyond the bounds of rational analysis. The topic, however, had particular attractions for me.

Firstly, as a farmer in Ireland and in a sense a pioneer who had operated a yard-and-milking shed system with a substantial dairy herd, I knew enough about livestock farming to understand most of the technical points involved. Secondly, the Irish study had alerted me to the close and often complex socio-economic relationships between livestock and people. No student of the Irish scene, for example, could be unaware of the often literally murderous competition between cattle and people for land in the 19th century. Sir Thomas More had protested about the English enclosures in the 16th century, that "sheep do eat up men"; while in 19th century Ireland the cry was "the land for the people, the road for the bullock". Finally, it became quickly apparent in the Third World that here was a very extensive yet largely untouched field of study that could reveal much about the human condition. Though normally dwarfed in terms of value of output by cropping, livestock worldwide occupied twice as much land as crops; and whereas any one crop, such as wheat or rice, was grown by only a proportion of cropgrowers on a small proportion of the world's total cropland, the keeping of cattle and buffaloes was practised universally and by more people than any other enterprise. Yet there had to date been no systematic study of the economics of the world's cattle and buffalo keeping.

As I observed at the beginning of this work, a different perspective may allow persons of unexceptional talents to acquire new and possibly useful insights. Being reared on the flagstones of Kilkenny's pavements contributed to my making the sort of farming mistakes of which anyone 'racey of the soil' could never be guilty. Those mistakes turned me to the study of the economics of agriculture in Ireland, a small country where the limits of such study were soon exhausted. Thus I found myself, an Irish agricultural economist, looking at the livestock problems of Malaysia, a country in South East Asia. Once having shifted from Ireland to Malaysia, it was easy and even natural to move on from there to the Caribbean and Latin America; and from there in turn to India and Africa. These largely fortuitous circumstances resulted in my being (a) a farmer with practical experience of livestock farming; (b) an economist with a special interest in the economic relationships between people and their livestock; and (c) an observer of all the major livestock keeping systems of the world. This was probably a unique combination of circumstances and yielded the sort of insights that would certainly never have occurred to me had I remained either in academic life or in Ireland. For to paraphrase: "What does he of Ireland know who only Ireland knows?"

The Disruption of Order

Everywhere in the Third World livestock production is in disarray. Old systems that had evolved to meet local circumstances and local needs are everywhere breaking down, though the manner of breakdown differs from region to region. In Malaysia and the other countries of South East Asia, where cattle and buffaloes are kept for draught and meat but not for milk, their numbers tend to decline. There is concern about this declining number of cattle and buffaloes, especially in view of the rapidly growing human population of the region. Reflecting that concern, every country in the region has laws prohibiting the slaughter of female cattle and buffaloes. But no more than it is possible to legislate prosperity into existence, laws cannot force people to have more buffaloes if there are compelling forces causing them to reduce their numbers.

I got a very clear insight into the nature of those forces in Kampong Pasir Salik, in the State of Perak, Malaysia (formerly Malaya). Kampong (or village) Pasir Salik is located in one of the most fertile and longest settled areas of Malayasia. It is distinguished as being the scene of the only fatality Britain suffered in the appropriation into the Empire of Malaya, one of the richest colonies. At one end of Kampong Pasir Salik, on the bank of the Perak river, is a modest column, with an English inscription (unintelligible to the villagers) dedicating it to the memory of John Birch, an Irishman in the service of the Malayan administration, who was killed in a skirmish on that spot in 1875, in the course of Britain's extension of its rule over the peninsula.

I came as near as I have ever been to meeting my Maker in the same Malay village as my fellow countryman, John Birch. I explained to some of the villagers that I had come to study why so much land that had previously been cropped with rubber and other tree crops had reverted to jungle. Or why, in a word, the villagers were so wretchedly poor? The reaction was quite out of character with the normally mild and gentle character of the Malays; though it should not have been so unexpected, as I had earlier read the inscription on the pillar. An angry murmur arose from the villagers and a number of the ubiquitous parangs, or cutlasses, used for cutting back the ever-encroaching tropical vegetation, became ominously visible. With the help of Ahmad, the Malay chap who was with me, and several bottles of orange squash bought from the sparsely stocked village shop, we got the matter sorted out. The villagers were fed up with people from one or other of the sixteen government quangoes operating in the region coming to survey and inquire about their poverty. They were tired of inquiries; now they wanted *maken*, or food for their empty bellies. Only then did I begin to realise the full extent of Malayan poverty, which is nevertheless mild by comparison with other Third World situations.

These Malay people were busy, at the beginning of this century, clearing the surrounding jungle and planting it to rubber trees. So effective were they in doing this that the British authorities positively discouraged them from rubber planting, an occupation that they prefered to reserve for British capital and management. But now the land that had once been under rubber had reverted to jungle, and the people were hungry. The explanation was interesting.

In 1875, when John Birch was martyred for the Empire, the total population of Malays was 500,000, of whom some 200 were in Kampong Pasir Salik. Now that population had increased tenfold to five million, with 2000 of them located in Kampong Pasir Salik. That population growth was brought about almost entirely by the introduction of very simple, very inexpensive sanitation measures which had first been practised in the West a century earlier. Applied in Malaya and other tropical countries, the effect was to slash death rates from around 50 per 1000 per annum to 20. Where population had been stable before, it now grew at over 2% annually and multiplied tenfold in a century.

The people of the kampong had cleared the jungle and planted it to rubber at an early stage in this process, when society was still stable and in balance. The balance may not have been ideal, being achieved mainly by a high death rate, especially among infants, but it was a balance. Seventy or eighty years on, that balance had been utterly disrupted. Output failed to keep up with population. Living and nutritional standards fell, but thanks to simple, inexpensive public sanitation measures, death rates continued below high birth rates and population continued to grow.

Because people were poorer, hungrier and less nourished, they were forced to concentrate their limited effort on activities that gave a quick return. Best preferred activity, because of the quick return, was daily or weekly wage work on nearby rubber estates or on public work schemes. Next best was rice-growing. But work on the villagers' own tree crops, including rubber, for which the climate is ideal, only yielded a return after a long time, and hungry people could not wait for that. They were forced to conserve what little energy their malnourished bodies could mobilise for work that gave an immediate return. This was why land that had been cleared from the jungle and planted in earlier, less stressful, times was now reverting to the jungle.

Tree crops were not all that suffered. In every society, however impoverished, there are wealthy people, often grown wealthy by impoverishing others. These elites in Malaysia were prepared to pay a high price for the meat of the buffaloes which the Malays used as draught animals to grow rice. Like desperately hungry people who eat the seed corn instead of planting it, the Malays were being forced by their poverty to cash in their buffaloes, even though this meant they would be unable to grow as much rice in future, and so must in time become even worse off. The Malays knew this as well as I or anyone else. But if a family is hungry and has no other income, it has little option but to relieve the pressing needs of the moment, whatever about the future.

The cattle/buffalo situation is very different in South Asia, or India. In South East Asia, where buffaloes are used for draught and their meat is eaten, the problem is one of declining bovine stocks. In India, where cattle and buffaloes are used for draught and milk, but are not eaten, the problem is one of ever worsening over-stocking. Eighteen per cent of the world's bovines are crowded on to India's two per cent of the world's farmland.

I began to understand India's problem of overstocking when observing Indian cowkeepers at work. The most skilful part of their work is to allow each calf at milking time to suckle its dam long enough to get sufficient milk to keep it alive till the next milking, but not a moment or a drop of milk longer. If the calf got less milk it died and the cow ceased to milk until it calved again in a year's time or longer. If the calf took more milk, there was less for the cowkeeper and his family. This was quite a different procedure from back on the farm in Dunbell. There the calves were taken from the cows at birth and sold by Biddy, my wife, often after hours of haggling on the doorstep. The Kerry cows, after an hour or so of distressful mooing, forgot about their calves and got on with the business of letting down their milk.

Then I learnt something that is not in any of the textbooks that I have read, yet is supremely important in the world's cattle economy. The world's cows come in two sorts: those that let down their milk whether or not their live calves are present (as the Kerries did); and cows that milk only if their live calves are present to suckle them. On inquiry, I discovered that all cows of the West are of the former type while all the cows of Africa and of most of Asia are of the latter sort.

This gives rise to a very remarkable situation. Every year about 20 million cows calve in India and the same number of calves are reared, to induce the cows to milk. This is recorded in India's livestock censuses which, like similar censuses in every country of the Empire, were started by the British; but which continue to be reliable only in India and Ireland. Also recorded in India's livestock censuses is the fact that there are only 10 million cattle aged 1 to 2 years, although 20 million calves are born and reared annually and no cattle are slaughtered in a country where beef-eating is taboo! Clearly what happens is that when the cows have ceased to milk, their calves, now around six months old, are put out to graze on what in Kilkenny is called "the long meadow" - or the roadside hedges. With so many animals to graze India's sunbaked "long meadows", the pickings are understandably poor; and the surprising thing is that even more than half the wretched animals do not perish during their first few months on it. India's agronomic and economic planners were astounded and initially incredulous when I brought these matters to their attention.

Tabooing the slaughter and consumption of cattle was a brilliant social innovation which gave India an abundance of draught animals. That abundance enables India to produce more food from its land surface than is produced from any comparable area of land in the world. But a high natural cattle mortality rate was crucial for keeping cattle numbers under control, given that their owners breed them as frequently as possible to induce lactation; that the calves had to be kept alive for the same purpose; that there is a taboo on cattle slaughter; and that all cattle are grazed communally on common land. However, just as medical science easily and cheaply slashed human mortality in South East Asia and caused a population explosion that utterly disrupted the former balance, so in India, the same influence, through veterinary science, has made it much more difficult for Indian cattle to die. Cattle stocks have become hopelessly excessive and the most ferocious starvation is now necessary to kill off ten million yearling cattle annually, which alone prevents numbers from rising to disastrously high levels.

In South America the situation in relation to cattle was very different from either India or South East Asia. Cattle, for starters, were still something of an innovation. There had been no cattle in North or South America 500 years ago, before

Columbus sailed the ocean blue
In fourteen hundred and ninety-two.

In the Old World, cattle had been closely integrated into

40

peoples' lives for millennia. Symbolic of that close relationship was the provision, two thousand years ago, of valuable warming services at Christmas in a stable in Bethlehem. Symbolic also of the relatively recent arrival of cattle in South America is the fact that most cattle there are owned by creoles, or people of exclusively or mainly European descent. Most of the indigenous population are as cattleless today as were their forebears 500 years ago.

South America has nearly four times as many cattle and two and a half times as much grazing land, per head of population, as the rest of the world has. Yet everywhere in South America cattle stocks tend to decline; consumption of beef is declining; and every country has the same sort of laws as in South East Asia against the slaughter of female cattle. These laws are as ineffective in South America as they are in South East Asia. Understandably, there is much concern in the region about the failure of cattle production to expand. That concern was shared by the agencies for which I worked in South America: the World Bank and the Commission of the Andean Pact – a South American equivalent of the EEC.

A low calving rate is part of the problem. About 45 cows per 100 calve annually, compared to around 90 per 100 in Ireland. Part of the reason for the low calving rate is the poor demand for milk in South America. The local people, like the Red Indians in North America and like all the peoples of East and South East Asia, are lactose malabsorbent; beyond infancy, they experience nausea and worse when they drink milk. Also, of the calves born, nearly half fail to reach maturity.

Intervention by the governments of the region, the World Bank, the Andean Pact and other aid agencies was mostly concerned to raise cow fertility and to reduce calf mortality. An encounter with some Italians in Bogota, the capital of Colombia, helped me to see why these efforts appeared to come to naught.

The Italians explained that they were in South America looking for young cattle for Italy's burgeoning cattle-fattening industry. Why in goodness' name did they not go to Ireland, where there were large numbers of excellent young cattle, located, from an Italian viewpoint, on the right side of the Atlantic Ocean? They had been there, but found that the

41

government banned the export of young cattle. Hence their trip to South America. (Subsequently I confirmed the existence of this export ban, which appeared to apply to only one other item: scrap-iron. The one ban was designed to ensure an abundant supply of inexpensive young cattle, produced mainly by small farmers, for fattening mainly by large farmers; and the other ban was designed to ensure a supply of low cost scrap-iron for Irish Steel.) The Italians figured that if they were allowed to export the young cattle from South America, they could get them to Italy at a cost that would make the operation worthwhile. The price of young cattle must be very low in South America.

The price of a 50kg calf in Ireland is around £200, or about 25% of the price of a 500kg fat animal. Cattle in South America are normally slaughtered at a much lower weight, around 300kg, though at a much older age: 5-6 years, compared to 2-3 years in Ireland. They were worth around 1000 pesos at slaughter. Insofar as I could gather, a calf in South America was worth around 20-30 pesos, or 2-3% of the value of a slaughter animal. Given that calves were virtually valueless and that people did not buy milk, it was understandable that little effort was made to breed cows in order to produce virtually valueless calves. And when the calves were produced, it was understandable that people did not trouble much to keep them alive. It was, on the other hand, equally understandable that cattle owners in South America would prefer to sell their heifers, even illegally, rather than breed to them to produce a succession of virtually valueless calves.

Having got this far, it was obvious that measures to raise cow fertility or reduce calf mortality were pointless in South America. The real problem was that it was not worth mating heifers to produce calves that were only worth 2-3% of the value of the heifers; and when those young calves were born, it was not worth keeping them alive. This had nothing to do with animal diseases, veterinary science or farm management. It had everything to do with the prevalence in South America of *reforma agraria,* or agrarian reform. South American *reforma agraria* is very like the agrarian outrage that was common in 19th century Ireland and that, for very understandable reasons, took the form of assassinating landlords and houghing cattle. Given the prevalence of *reforma agraria* in South America, it is small wonder that, though six year old cattle are worth 1000 pesos, calves are worth only 20 pesos.

Africa was the last major cattle-keeping region in the Third World which I had an opportunity to study. A pattern had begun to emerge by that stage. Unlike the Old World, cattle in South America were a relatively recent innovation and were used there for meat only. By contrast, traditionally in Europe cattle had been used for meat, for milk and for draught. But in East and Southeast Asia, they were used only for draught and meat, not for milk. In India, they were used for draught and milk, but not for meat. And now in Africa, I realised that cattle were used for milk and meat, but not for draught. Africa's failure to use its cattle for draught very largely accounts for the fact that this continent, with half as many people and six times more land, feeds its people much worse than India.

As in India, Africa's cattle economy was ruined by overstocking. I had an opportunity to see on a piece of rehabilitated land what Africa's grazing land must have been like a century ago. This was land that, with reasonable management, would well carry an animal to two acres. Such has been the destruction caused by overgrazing, African cattle now barely survive at one animal per five acres. The entire continent is being turned into desert, with the Kalahari expanding from the south to meet the Sahara which is expanding from the north.

Like most people, I had heard about the overstocking of Africa's grazing land. But I only appreciated its severity when I saw cattle on the utterly bare, thorn-infested grazing land of Kwa Zulu, that part of South Africa which is the homeland of the Zulu people. These were cattle so emaciated by starvation that a good push would knock any of them, and few would ever rise again. One never sees anything like this state of emaciation here because few of those cattle would survive an Irish October, and none of them would survive an Irish winter. One needed to be on the spot to realize that Africa's typically warm weather allows cattle to survive with virtually nothing to graze but thorn bushes. Indeed, about the only thing that kills cattle in

Africa is drought when watering holes dry up in dry seasons.

The overgrazing was perhaps worse in Kwa Zulu than in the rest of Africa. This is because the South African-maintained veterinary services are better there. For example, every animal was supposed to be – and most were – dipped weekly against tick-born diseases. It therefore took more overgrazing and more starvation to kill off enough cattle to maintain a stable cattle population.

Starvation as a means of balance is all the more unavoidable because the other great traditional controller of cattle numbers went out with the major cattle diseases. Western law and order put an end to cattle-raiding at the same time as western veterinary science put an end to the major livestock diseases. It was because, in pre-European times, Africans were so busy raiding and killing their neighbours' cattle, or defending their own, that they made no use of the cattle for draught. (The pre-Conquest Irish also made little use of their cattle for draught, for the same reason: they were too busy mounting or repelling cattle raids, known in Gaelic as *creagh,* pronounced crack.)

Not surprisingly, as the land deteriorates and the animals become increasingly unproductive and emaciated, they also become increasingly disease and pest-ridden. Ever increasing quantities of veterinary services and medicines are necessary in order to keep the diseases and parasites at bay. This leads to an unceasing and pointless struggle between the diseases and parasites on the one hand, and the veterinary services and medicines that gave rise to the overstocking in the first instance. As Africa's cattle-keeping becomes ever more unproductive, it becomes ever more dependent on those western influences that made it unproductive in the first instance. Too readily the western countries supply the veterinary services and medicine which ensure that overstocking and over-grazing persist as surely as pouring petrol on a fire ensures continued combustion. Ireland, posing as a "developed" country concerned to develop the poorer countries no less than the rest, indulges in this inanity. Supplying veterinary services to Africa is one of the principal ways in which the Irish Department of Foreign Affairs spends the money of Irish taxpayers to "help" the people of poorer countries.

"Operation Flood"

Most of the "aid" given by Ireland and other countries for livestock development in Africa is in the form of veterinary services and medicines. But this is only part of a much more general, continued western intervention which, under the guise of helping the Third World, really benefits major interests in the West (like the suppliers of veterinary services and medicines) and in the Third World, while simultaneously wreaking great harm on the poor of the Third World. "Operation Flood" is an important case in point.

India's Operation Flood is an illustration, from a quite different cultural background, of the manner in which native governments, the governments of donor countries and the international development agencies by their actions exacerbate the problems arising from the disarray of traditional livestock-keeping systems. Largely because of the disarray caused originally by western influences, the cost of milk relative to the price of labour is nearly fifty times higher in India than in the West. There is understandably a strong demand in India for milk which, in a largely vegetarian society, is effectively the only source of animal protein. Demand is especially strong among the relatively wealthy urban population. Virtually any scheme to increase the supply of milk in India would therefore appear to be desirable. This was especially the case with Operation Flood - to "flood" India with milk, as Jim Dillon in 1948 threatened to flood England with Irish eggs.

Operation Flood was based on the use of EEC dairy surpluses, which had already become a serious problem in 1970, as food aid for India. The manner of its use by Operation Flood countered the serious objection that had been registered against other forms of food aid. The disposal of surpluses by the USA and other countries that were burdened with excess agricultural stocks, especially of grain, frequently harmed recipient countries. This was principally because acceptance by those countries of agricultural commodities like grain depressed the price of these to their own producers. To the extent that it did so, it discouraged production and hence created in the recipient countries a condition of perpetual dependence.

That could not be said of Operation Flood, which was designed to increase milk production in India. The EEC's surplus butter and skimmed milk powder (smp) is delivered free under Operation Flood to the Indian National Dairy Corporation (INDC). The INDC reconstitutes these and sells the resulting milk in the major cities. With the proceeds it is able to pay a higher price for more milk in the villages, which it then takes to the cities, sometimes over distances of 500 kilometres.

So far so good. Everyone appears to benefit. Embarrassing EEC dairy surpluses, which are costly to store, are disposed of otherwise than by sale at give-away prices to the Russians, which evokes howls of protest from EEC consumers and tax-payers and from competing dairy exporters in the USA and New Zealand. India's urban consumers benefit from getting more milk, some of it reconstituted EEC milk and some produced locally in response to the higher price which the INDC can pay. Indian milk producers benefit from the higher prices paid by the INDC. And of course EEC milk producers have benefited greatly too. Without Operation Flood and the hundreds of thousands of tonnes it has taken off the butter and skimmed milk powder mountains, the imposition of a quota system for EEC milk producers would have come sooner and the quotas would have been smaller.

But there are snags. These are not obvious to the vast majority of people who are unaware of the peculiarities of milk production in India. The snags can also easily be ignored by the many who profit from Operation Flood and have no desire to see its unattractive aspects.

The first of these is that Operation Flood raises - and is designed to raise - the price of milk in the villages and rural areas where it is produced. But most of the inhabitants of those areas, who comprise the majority of Indians and who are among the world's poorest, are too poor to have cows. They are not producers but consumers of milk whenever their pitifully low incomes allow them to buy a cupful of a food for which their protein-starved bodies crave. By making it more difficult for them to buy milk, one effect of Operation Flood is seriously to damage hundreds of millions of the world's poorest, least articulate and most defenceless people.

Secondly Operation Flood, by raising the price paid to Indian producers for milk, makes it more attractive for them to keep cows. Producers respond by attempting to increase further the share of the world's bovines, already 18%, crowded on to India's 2% of the world's farmland. To the extent that they succeed, Operation Flood exacerbates the underlying problem of overstocking, which in India and Africa has been caused by western influences.

Finally, Operation Flood raises the price of milk relative to the price of grain in India. Reflecting the disarray of cattle-keeping in the country, a disarray which is common to all capitalist colonized Third World countries, the price of milk is high relative not only to wages but to the price of grains. A gallon of milk is worth twice as much grain in India as in the West, including even the EEC where the price of milk is exceptionally high and well above anything that might be described as an economic price. Because of its relatively high value, virtually all milk in India is produced from crop products, rather than from pasture as in Ireland. (Indeed, in all Third World countries, commercial milk production is similarly based. Milk producers in these countries find it difficult to understand why the price of milk is so high in Ireland, where virtually all feeding comes from grazing.) A higher milk price, which Operation Flood causes, therefore makes it more profitable to feed more grain to cows to produce more milk. In this way, the EEC and its member states are subsidising the diversion of grain from the bellies of hundreds of millions of malnourished Indians into the bellies of cows producing milk for the relatively wealthy among the urban population.

Operation Flood, on which both the EEC and the World Bank have spent several hundred millions of dollars since its inception in 1972, so far from being a model for the development of a Third World cattle industry is in fact perfectly designed to benefit powerful, wealthy interests while simultaneously doing harm to great numbers of poor people who because of their poverty are weak, inarticulate and unable to defend themselves.

I first expressed these criticisms in an article in *The Times* of London in May 1976. Subsequently I made representations about them to the Commission of the EEC in Brussels and to the Advisory Council for Development Cooperation (ACDC). The ACDC is an Irish semi-state body comprising representatives of various vocational groupings, including agriculture, the trade unions and business, which is intended to advise government on the allocation of public resources for aid to Third World countries. Although the Irish government has spent some 10% of its total development funds on Operation Flood, more than on any other project, the ACDC chose to ignore the criticisms made of the exercise. Apparently the vested interests of the farmers producing the dairy surpluses, and of the trade unions with members working in the creameries, overrode consideration of the harm being done to India's poor by the dumping in India of surplus Irish dairy produce.

A number of European non-governmental organisations involved in aid to the Third World have since become aware of the harm being done by Operation Flood to India's poor. Several Indian academics and journalists also interested themselves in the matter and through their investigations of the project on the spot revealed the flaws in it which the EEC, the World Bank and the Irish ACDC had chosen to ignore. As a result of sustained and mounting criticism by these groups, both in India and Europe, the EEC has recently decided to end its involvement in Operation Flood.

A Synthesis of Experiences

Long before I left Aberystwyth, it had become clear that though the land question and the associated agricultural failure were central to the poor performance of the Irish economy, this was by no means the whole story. In a sense, these matters were merely symptomatic of a deeper, more fundamental malaise that affected the whole Irish body politic. Until that malaise was understood and treated, there was no prospect of improving the Irish situation, or any component part of it. These ideas remained with me in the new life of economic advisor in the Third World.

As I became acquainted with, and achieved what appeared

to be important new insights into, the problems of pastoral resource use in the Third World, my other and abiding interest in Ireland progressed also. There was an interaction or "feedback" between the two lines of inquiry: Ireland's poor economic performance and the disarray in the use of grazing land and animals in the Third World. There was in both cases a failure to mobilize resources effectively for the social wellbeing.

My more recent enquiry into the misuse of pastoral resources was global in extent; the older, but continuing enquiry into the Irish conditions, was narrower and more limited in scope, but more deep-reaching. The deeper insights gained from the older Irish enquiry suggested hypotheses and questions to pursue in the new pastoral resource use enquiry. The more generalized results achieved from the pastoral enquiry helped to place the Irish enquiry into a much broader and intellectually suggestive context.

I slowly came to realise that there was much in common between the failure of the Irish to secure a livelihood in Ireland and the widespread, growing and worsening poverty of the Third World. Fewer people get a livelihood in Ireland now than at any time in the past 250 years. More people in the Third World now experience worse poverty than ever before. In both cases there is a growing disparity between what is supplied and what is required. In the one case the disparity is reflected in broadening, worsening poverty; in the other it is reflected in half the population stream departing to get abroad the livelihood that is denied to them in Ireland. True, living standards are rising in Ireland and have been for 140 years. But the higher standards have been available only to a declining number of people. If, for example, the population of India had changed over the past 140 years in the same way as Ireland's, India would now have 60 million people instead of 600 million. With a population of 60 million and a unified internal market, India might now well be one of the wealthiest rather than one of the poorest countries in the world.

By contrast with those Irish and more general Third World conditions, in other countries there are more people than ever before enjoying higher living standards and fewer people experiencing poverty as bad as in the past. That does not by any means imply that Utopia reigns in all or any of these countries; it is all too easy, in the USA for example, to point to pockets of poverty and human degradation almost as bad as in the past. But these pockets are much more circumscribed than formerly; they are the more obvious because of their contrast with the more general and substantial improvement; and they merely verify in a very limited sense the ancient verity: "the poor you have always with you". Even in the most prosperous and equitable societies, there will be some who fail to cope. The presence of such pockets of distress, in the USA, Britain or the USSR cannot take from the substantial achievement of these countries:

a) in supporting more people who are better off than at any time in the past;

and

b) in having fewer people who are as badly off now as in the past.

To refer to these countries as "developed" seems akin to speaking of an individual as "good". Complacency, self-satisfaction, an assumption of the existence of Utopia and the suggestion that even pockets of social stress no longer exist seem to be implied by the term, "developed". For these reasons, "developing" appears to be a more appropriate term. The countries concerned are moving in the general direction of Utopia, but have not reached it yet.

In the other countries one or other of the two basic conditions for development does not exist. Taking India as an important example: many more people there are better off now than at any time in the past. There are, for example, in India 60 million people whose average incomes are as high as those of France, which has a total population of 55 million and has one of the highest average income levels in Europe. India therefore fulfils the first condition for developing. But what of the second? The fact is that there are hundreds of millions of people existing in India now at lower income levels than ever before. Previously such people would long since – at birth mainly – have been killed off by disease, as cattle were traditionally in Africa. But now, thanks to the practice of the elementary principles of public hygiene and preventive medicine, the great killer diseases of the past no longer operate so effectively and people in large numbers subsist at living standards that would have been impossible in the past.

Ireland also fails to fulfil both of the conditions of development specified above. But it does so in a unique fashion. Unlike India and other Third World countries, Ireland has now fewer people who are as badly off as in the past and therefore fulfills condition (b); but again unlike India, Ireland has fewer people who are as well off now as in the past - condition (a) above. This is because Ireland, as already mentioned, now has fewer people able to get a livelihood than at any time in the past 250 years.

As it seems appropriate to describe fulfilling both conditions set out above as "developing" rather than the more common "developed", so it seems more true to refer to countries failing to fulfil both of the conditions as "undeveloping" rather than "developing". "Developing" implies that while conditions are not satisfactory, the countries are moving in the general direction of improvement. That palpably is not so. It cannot be sensibly regarded as an improvement that India has now perhaps 40 million people who are better off and 400 million who are worse off than when the British raj ended forty years ago. Neither can it be regarded as an improvement that there are fewer people living in slums in Ireland and 250,000 fewer people in the work force and able to get a livelihood in Ireland now than when the British left sixty-five years ago.

It is therefore possible to dichotomize the countries of the world into those that are developing and those that are undeveloping. Looking more closely at that dichotomy, it is seen that *all the countries that are developing have not been capitalist colonized; while all the countries that are undeveloping have been capitalist colonized.*

"Capitalist colonized" refers to a situation where during the past 500 years one or other of the following European countries – Spain, Portugal, The Netherlands, Britain, France, Denmark, Belgium, Germany, or Italy – established sovereignty over another territory and ruled the food producing peoples of those other territories for the profit of capitalists in the metropoles. It is distinguished from the other "settler colonization", which occurred during the same period

51

and which also involved Europeans occupying territories, but territories which had previously been held by hunters and gatherers, notably in North America, Australia and New Zealand. The indigenes in these latter settler colonies were not – could not have been – "squeezed" for metropolitan profit. They were for the most part exterminated.

Once the identification has been recognized between capitalist colonization and undevelopment and not being capitalist colonized and development, the question naturally arises as to the mechanism whereby this identification is achieved. No crude explanation of continuing exploitation of the former colonies by the former metropolitan powers, often referred to as neo-colonialism, could be held plausibly to account for the identifications. This was particularly so as undevelopment appeared to proceed if anything at an accelerating pace after independence. And after all, some undeveloping former capitalist colonies – those of Latin America – have been independent for 160 years and more. Ireland has been independent for 65 years. Some undeveloping African countries, like Kenya, have now been independent for as long as they were colonies.

The global study on pastoral resource use seemed to throw light on the problem. All the countries studied were former capitalist colonies. They included Ireland, where the conflict between people and cattle has been noted. Common to all these situations was the experience of having had superimposed on their indigenous culture, in the process of capitalist colonization, western culture pertaining to pastoral resource use. In Ireland and the other former capitalist colonies of the Old World, that western culture was imposed on an indigenous pastoral resource use system which had previously evolved in response to local circumstances. One important element of that new, superimposed culture was the question of the ownership of livestock and of the land they grazed; another was veterinary medicine. In Latin America, as noted, everything pertaining to pastoral resource use originated with the Iberian powers which colonized the region and introduced cattle and sheep there as well as the *latifundia* system, or an oligarchy of large landowners and a mass of propertyless peons.

Two sets of interlinked ideas thus evolved in tandem. First,

Irish economic failure was perceived increasingly to be part of a much broader pattern of the undevelopment of all the former capitalist colonies. There are some 140 of these, containing in all some 2000 million people. None of them has succeeded in transforming undevelopment into the development that is characteristic of all the other, non-capitalist-colonized countries of the world, even though some of them, as noted, have been independent for a century longer than Ireland. The second line of thought was that western culture, out of context in undeveloping former capitalist colonies, invariably brought about disarray in local pastoral resource use. The disarray took different forms according to the local culture; but it had a common origin – the impact, out of context, of western institutions and technology.

After grappling with these problems for almost a decade while working as an economic consultant and at the same time pursuing independent research on the Irish scene, I needed to work out and to publish my ideas. A choice was necessary between a more narrowly based Irish study or a more general, global pastoral resource use study. To speak of "a crisis" in Ireland in 1975 was to evoke the response "what crisis?". The oil crisis of 1974 had been taken by the Irish economy in its stride. Growth was at a record rate; and the long established flow of emigration had been reversed into net immigration. The numbers at work, having declined virtually non-stop since the 1840s, had begun to increase. The Whitakerian era of economic miracles had not yet ended in Ireland, and book publishers were not interested in books about an Irish economic crisis.

The situation with regard to Third World pastoral resource use was a little more promising. Development agencies like the World Bank had for some time been directing an increasing part of their attention towards securing the development of the Third World's pastoral resources. There was a growing appreciation among them of the enormous extent of those resources in the Third World and of the abysmally poor returns secured from them. The governments of many Third World countries had themselves begun to attempt to improve the productivity of their pastoral resources. They were receiving increasing support from the various development agencies for this. Typical of all this was the increase in loans for livestock projects by the World Bank from 32 in 1970 to 68 in 1976. This represented an increase from 13% to 17% of World Bank lending to agriculture in those years.

But neither the governments of the Third World nor the development agencies were being successful in their efforts to increase the output of pastoral products. Indeed, to a very great extent, those efforts were exacerbating the very conditions they were purportedly intended to rectify. And that is not surprising. Governments respond to pressure. People can exert pressures in proportion to their wealth. Governments are therefore most responsive to the pressures exerted by the rich and least responsive to the pressures exerted by the poor.

International aid-giving agencies and the aid-giving activities of donor countries, including the Irish Department of Foreign Affairs, operate in Third World countries in collaboration with, and through, the governments of those countries. Understandably then, development efforts in the Third World, whether undertaken by the governments of the countries concerned or financed from abroad, are influenced by the views and aspirations of the wealthy rather than by those of the poor. To that extent these development efforts tend to make the rich richer and the poor poorer.

The provision of veterinary services and medicines to Africa, and India's Operation Flood, illustrate the manner in which continued western intervention exacerbates the problems caused originally by western capitalist colonialism. An integral part of the disruption of traditional African cattlekeeping is the tremendous concentration of cattle ownership that has occurred. Traditionally, there were no "cattle barons" and no cattleless people in Africa. Now the situation as I found it in a part of Kwa Zulu is typical of Africa as a whole. One powerful individual owned half the cattle; about 10% of households owned the remainder; and 90% of the households had no cattle. The cattle-owning elites throughout Africa create the demand for veterinary services and medicines, which Ireland and other western countries provide readily. That "aid" is a chief cause of the continuing disintegration of traditional African cattle husbandry.

In India, there has been effective support from the urban

elite milk consumers, from the rural landowners, and especially from the bureaucracy in the National Dairy Corporation for western involvment. It is to the demands of these elements that the Irish government listens when it gives 10% of its foreign aid to Operation Flood. The suffering caused to India's inarticulate masses is conveniently ignored.

A visiting fellowship at the Institute of Development Studies at the University of Sussex in 1976 gave me the opportunity to think out the problem of the hopelessly unproductive use of the vast resources of grazing land and domestic grazing animals throughout the Third World. Although the land involved accounted for two thirds of all the world's agricultural land, and although more people worked with cattle than were involved in any other productive enterprise in the world, very little study had been done on the subject. Agronomists, who knew about cattle, tended to take a narrowly technical view of the problems involved and saw the way ahead in terms of such technical innovations as artificial insemination of local stock by bulls of more productive western cattle stock. Economists, who generally know little about cattle, largely ignored the subject. Sociologists tended to study the subject piecemeal and, while frequently producing revealing insights into particular aspects, had done little by way of securing an overall view of the problem.

Differences between cattle-keeping conditions in the West and in the Third World, and between different parts of the Third World, are deeply embedded in ecological, historical and socio-economic and even genetic origins. Two of these differences, the results of millennia of genetic evolution, have already been noted. First, all the breeds of cows in the West are, like the Kerries which I had in Dunbell, of the *Bos taurus* type, which let down their milk with or without the presence of their live calves: while the cows of Africa and India are of the *Bos indicus* type, which lactate only in the presence of their live calves. Second, thousands of years of genetic evolution have resulted in high proportions of adult Africans, Europeans and Indians being able to consume milk - they are lactose tolerant. On the other hand, nearly all adult East and South-

East Asians and indigenous Americans cannot consume milk-they are lactose malabsorbent.

Transfers of institutions and technology between one cattle-keeping culture and another must obviously, therefore, be undertaken with care and consideration to avoid disrupting indigenous systems that have evolved slowly through the ages to meet local circumstances, and that are often fragile. In practice what has happened is that the West introduces the institutions and technology from which it profits, regardless of their local impact. Ireland supplies veterinary services to Africa and dairy surpluses to India through Operation Flood for the benefit of Irish interests, without knowing or caring about their effect on the peoples of Africa and India. Complementing those elements in the West which seek to profit by injecting Western influences into the cattle-keeping systems of the Third World, there are in the Third World individual and sectional interests, such as the cattle-owning elites of Africa and Latin America and the National Dairy Corporation in India, which profit locally by the acceptance and application of those Western influences.

The final result of this pursuit of selfish interest by elements in both the West and the Third World is the sort of utter disruption of Third World pastoral resource use already emphasized. A measure of that disruption is that whereas the cropland of poor countries yields two-thirds as much per acre as cropland in the wealthy countries, the pastureland of the poor countries yields less than one-fifth as much per acre and the cattle yield only one-twelfth as much per head. Without £1 more investment, or the slightest technological innovation, but simply by curbing the selfish interests in the West as well as in the Third World which have caused, and continue to cause, the disruption of the Third World's use of pastoral resources, the output of milk and meat from these resources could be multiplied manifold. It would not end, but it would greatly alleviate, want and malnutrition in the Third World.

These were the ideas I worked on and developed while at the Institute of Development Studies at Sussex University. They are expressed in my book *Cattle, Economics and Development*, published by the Commonwealth Agricultural Bureaux in 1980.

CHAPTER 3

Irish Undevelopment Revisited

Our Enemy the State

In 1982 a position in Trinity College, Dublin afforded me the opportunity to return to Ireland, which I had left in 1974, and to continue to work on the Irish economy. That economy had since palpably deteriorated and there might now be a readier acceptance of ideas I had been developing and advancing since turning from active farming to academic work nearly thirty years earlier.

It was now clear to me that the failure of the Irish economy, and particularly the denial of a livelihood to almost half the people born in Ireland, was part of a much wider failure. That wider failure is the persistent inability of the peoples of all the former capitalist colonies, together accounting for nearly half the world's population, to secure a livelihood. The Irish situation could only be understood in that broader context, which alone gave a proper perception of the complexity and intractability of the problems involved.

The Irish situation of course differs from that of the other former capitalist colonies, commonly referred to collectively as the Third World, but the differences are superficial rather than fundamental. They arise entirely from Ireland's European location and, as a consequence of that location, from Ireland's people being of the same Indo-European race as the peoples of the nine colonizing powers. This has led to the integration of that half of the Irish population who have been made economically surplus by capitalist colonialism and its heritage, into the colonizing system itself. They have been integrated as workers in metropolitan Britain, as soldiers, priests, nuns and so forth in the other capitalist colonies, or as settlers in the

57

settler colonies of North America and Oceania. That, in turn, made Irish incomes independent of the Irish economy, the performance of which determined only how many Irish could get a living in Ireland at those exogenously determined incomes. Relatively high incomes and the political stability resulting from them and from the emigration of the less contented half of six generations were the conditions that have made it possible for the Irish state to borrow more money relative to GNP than any other state in the world, and three times as much as Peru, the Latin American country with the relatively largest public debt. Underneath these differences lies the failure, common and peculiar to all former capitalist colonies, to mobilize resources so as to meet the needs of their people.

Every country that has not been capitalist colonized develops, regardless of whether it is market oriented (U.S.A.) or centrally planned (U.S.S.R.); Western (Germany) or Eastern (Japan); large (Canada) or small (Singapore). Every one of the 140 or so former capitalist colonies, containing in all some two billion people, undevelops, although some of these – those in Latin America – have been independent for a century longer than Ireland; and some of them are centrally planned (India and Tanzania) while others are market oriented (Kenya and Indonesia).

The closest analogy that occurs to me for the persistent undevelopment of the former capitalist colonies comes from the very first days after forsaking the pavement flags of Kilkenny for the fields of nearby Threecastles. Working with a horse and cart, I tied the horse loosely to a railings on one occasion. Returning a few minutes later, I found the horse, bending down to nibble some grass, had entangled the loose reins in its harness. In raising its head, the reins tightened on the bit, causing the horse to back away from the railings. Because now the reins were looped incorrectly around the harness, every movement backwards of the horse tightened still further the pull on the bit, causing the horse to try harder to move further back. The control system had gone haywire and only the immediate cutting of the reins avoided disaster. In every former capitalist colony in which I have worked, including Ireland, the economic control systems are similarly malfunctioning. We work harder and work ourselves out of jobs. We invest more in labour-saving, job-destroying plans. We educate our people better, for employment abroad by foreign producers of goods and services competing with Irish products.

The control system in question is the state which, through the institutions it maintains, the services it provides and the taxes it levies, determines the manner in which economies function. The state in every former capitalist colony causes the economic system to malfunction; those systems function sufficiently well in all countries that have not been capitalist colonized, at least to allow those countries to develop. The explanation for the different results secured by the control systems lies in the distinctive origin and nature of the state in former capitalist colonies.

The state in every former capitalist colony traces its lineaments directly to the administration established there for the purpose of exploiting the colony for metropolitan profit. In Ireland the state functions from the mile square surrounding Dublin Castle, the original centre of English rule in Ireland. Latin American states operate within the boundaries of the administrative provinces of the Spanish and Portuguese Empires. The boundaries of the African states are those arranged by the capitalist colonial powers at the Conference of Berlin in 1885 for their convenience, without regard to physical features or the dispositions of the African tribes, races and cultures.

Capitalist colonial administrations operated on the basis of privilege with its corresponding disability. The function of the state in all former capitalist colonies has been to maintain that privilege and associated disability. Privilege is defined as rights exercised without commensurate responsibility to the society within which the rights are exercised. They are pre-eminently rights enjoyed by a garrison class in return for services rendered to a capitalist colonial power. The epitome of capitalist colonial privilege is landed property, or the exclusive title by some to the land on which all depend for their existence. Landed property owes its origin in every former capitalist colony to the colonial regime. It is by far the most important form of property in all former capitalist colonies;

and, apart from the special case of England which I have dealt with in *Ireland in Crisis,* it is the most important form of property only in them. It is the principal part of the capitalist colonial heritage.

Capitalist colonial administrations established, preserved and expanded privilege, and corresponding disability, in the interest of the metropolitan powers. Decolonization in all cases has been a process of indigenizing privilege. Local interests, in the course of capitalist evolution, participated in privilege and eventually appropriated it from the metropolitan interest which originated and originally monopolized it. Thus Irish Catholic grazier farmers acquired from Anglo-Irish Protestant landlords the land which, at the original conquest, was confiscated from the clans. Similarly, Irish Catholics secured from Anglo-Irish Protestant bankers control of the money supply which, in a market economy, gave effective control of the stock of capital.

Independence has, in every former capitalist colony, been sought and secured by the privileged indigenous groups which emerged as part of the process of capitalist evolution. The chief concern of the indigenous privileged groups who secured independence has in every case been to enhance and to consolidate privilege. This has been done in part by recognizing and paying deference to local, nationalist feelings, by such gestures as painting red letter-boxes green, or commencing and ending official communications in the national language, and by playing a national instead of a metropolitan anthem. More substantively, metropolitan originating privilege/disability has been preserved and enhanced by a sufficient local extension of privilege to ensure sufficient political support for its retention in the post colonial era. The post capitalist colonial state has in every case been the agency for achieving this.

The state in every country that has not been capitalist colonized, by contrast, has evolved in diverse ways in response to diverse circumstances, but always in response to local needs. The state in every such country, though often subjected to intense outside pressures, has never sought to uphold institutions and practices that were designed and imposed originally to extract profit from its citizens for the benefit of non-citizens.

The independent state in every former capitalist colony preserves and enhances indigenous privilege at the cost of national undevelopment. It does so by using, in the same manner, the same institutions and technologies as were employed by its forerunner, the metropolitan administration, for the same purposes. These institutions (principally property) and the technologies (principally medical science) are not inherently socially destructive. It is the manner of their application, out of context, in former capitalist colonies that causes undevelopment.

The institutions and technologies in question evolved spontaneously in the very distinctive environment of Central Western Europe, where they were a critical element in the original development of that region. They have been applied subsequently with great success in the settler colonies of North America and Oceania, but they were applied there in effectively virgin territories from which the indigenous hunter-gatherers had been virtually obliterated, and so did not interact with the new culture. The institutions, and more so the technology, of the West have also been adopted by the countries of east Europe, especially Russia, and by those of east Asia. None of these countries was ever capitalist colonized and so they develop. Because the countries of east Europe and east Asia were not capitalist colonized, they were able to adopt western institutions and technology eclectically and adjust them to meet local needs.

The primary, specific manner in which the state in all former capitalist colonies perpetuates privilege/disability is through its determination of factor prices. The state determines the cost of land, capital and labour for producers at levels which maximize privilege and its associated disability, and without reference to economic realities.

The state in former capitalist colonies makes land free for the privileged who possess it. Because land is free, it is used inefficiently by its possessors and the nation languishes. Because the nation languishes, the disinherited, who could use land efficiently, are impoverished and cannot acquire land from the privileged. Thus Irish land, which relative to GNP is the most highly priced in the world, is used even more inefficiently than in most former capitalist colonies, where universally land is badly used and people are hungry.

The state in former capitalist colonies makes savings available free to politicians and free, or almost free, to the privileged. It does so by expanding the money supply and by public sector borrowing. The Irish state has secured control over, and used in these ways, far more savings relative to GNP than the state in any other former capitalist colony.

The state has suffered the banking system to expand the money supply from £150 millions 30 years ago to nearly £16 billions now. Through the Whitaker expedient of subsidising exports and capital inflows, it has managed so far to maintain, more or less, the convertibility of the currency. The Irish state has, over forty years, created a public debt of some £26 billions, or the equivalent of 160% of GNP.

These resources are the savings of the public, secured more or less voluntarily through state loans and involuntarily through inflation. They have been used in the first instance to maintain in power politicians whose primary concern has been to secure re-election, and control of the state; and to found political dynasties that preserve power for the grandchildren of the Republic's founding fathers. In my native constituency of Carlow-Kilkenny, all five sitting TDs are the sons of TDs.

After their use to sustain in office a corrupt, inequitable and inefficient political establishment, the voluntary and forced savings of the citizens have been made available free, or virtually free, to the privileged. The privileged have used the savings for three anti-social purposes. They have used them first to buy out competing firms, so as to make Irish business extremely and exceptionally monopolistic and uncompetitive. The privileged have used the citizens' savings secondly to acquire labour-replacing plant. Guinness, for example, have spent hundreds of millions of pounds of these free or virtually free savings on plant that enables them to produce, at their St. James's Gate brewery, the same amount of stout, of the same quality, at the same price, but with 1500 people instead of the 3500 who used to work there. By using more of these savings of the citizens, made available to it free or virtually free, Guinness expects presently to reduce its workforce further to 800 people.

The third, and final, use that the privileged make of the

citizens' savings is to invest them abroad. In Guinness's case, these have been used mainly for the illegal and fraudulent acquisition of the UK United Distillers Company. All the other major Irish companies, including Cement Roadstone, Smurfit, Creans, Waterford Glass, Independent Newspapers and Allied Irish Banks, operate on similar lines. Between them, they are now exporting savings secured voluntarily or involuntarily from Irish citizens at the rate of £600 million annually.

The state, while making land free for its privileged possessors, and capital free to politicians and virtually free to privileged borrowers, enormously raises the cost of labour. Because of high marginal tax rates, at the relatively modest salary of £12,750 per annum, it costs an employer in Ireland now £4.08 to place an additional £1 net of PAYE and PRSI deductions in an employee's pocket. Of that residual £1, the state takes another 15p in VAT on the employee's purchases. Thus to enable a worker to buy goods and services for which producers receive 85p, an employer, who can be the worker if he or she is self-employed, must pay the worker almost five times as much.

Individuals respond to this economically irrational (though politically rational) pricing system in a predictable, rational manner. In an economy where people for centuries have been killing one another to get possession of a patch of land; where the best brains in the civil service scrounge capital from the four corners of the globe; and where for nearly two centuries only half the labour force has been employed – in this economy, the sole measure of productivity is output per person. Output per acre or per unit of capital is ignored. This is a rational response by producers to a situation where the state has made land and capital virtually free for the privileged and has simultaneously made labour impossibly dear.

It is understandable, in these circumstances, that half the supply of Irish labour has never been used at all. The disability corresponding to the privileged access by some to free land and to free or virtually free capital is that half the nation are denied an opportunity to use their labour, because its cost has been raised so high by the state. That the Irish state operates in this manner stems from the fact that it owes its origin to a colonial administration which was established to exploit the nation. It is a state which continues to exploit the vast, deprived bulk of the members of the nation. It is a state which, as is the case with all the states in all the former capitalist colonies, is the enemy of the people and the nation.

A Unique Situation

Ireland moves rapidly into the eye of a crisis. It is a crisis such as distinguishes one epoch from the next, comparable to that which affected Ireland in the decades 1820-1850. The principal elements of the present crisis are uncannily similar to those of the earlier one.

Ireland in 1820 had acquired a social structure that was no longer compatible with the institutional framework that had been imposed upon it by capitalist colonialism. That social structure had evolved during the reign of a single English monarch, George III, from 1760 to 1820, in response to three sets of conditions: first, the market demands created by the early English industrial revolution; second, an agriculture that was distinguished by the combination of the lowest temperatures and highest rainfall anywhere in the world where extensive cropgrowing was attempted; and third, by an institutional framework whereby the operators of land had access to it only by paying its proprietors rack rents. In response to that unique set of circumstances, a class of coolies had emerged and become numerically the largest class in Ireland. This they did some 30 degrees of latitude further from the equator than any similar class elsewhere in the world. These were people who depended for their existence on crop growing, with few assets other than a spade and a few buckets of seed potatoes.

Given the institutional arrangements, especially that the purpose of land is to yield a profit to its proprietors rather than to sustain its inhabitants, the coolies, the largest social class in Ireland, were doubly vulnerable. The need for their services, and hence their ability to get access to land, depended upon the particular pattern of demand for Irish agricultural produce. With a new phase of industrialization, which commenced with the end of the Napoleonic wars in 1815, demand shifted from the labour-intensive commodities, grain and butter, to the labour-extensive commodities, cattle and sheep. Reflecting that fundamental, long run change in demand, the price of cattle in Ireland rose fivefold relative to grain and threefold relative to butter between 1820 and 1970.

The coolies, the largest social class in Ireland in 1820, were vulnerable too in their dependence on potatoes. The potato was the principal item in the diet of virtually all the people and was the sole item in the diet of half the people. This exotic crop from the Altiplano of South America had been introduced to Ireland a couple of centuries earlier; and had been a rarity until a little more than a century before it had become the principal item in the diet of the nation.

There is now an incongruity in Irish society quite as remarkable as that of the period 1820-1850. Today's incongruity is that Ireland has the values and aspirations of the developing West while it has the economy of the undeveloping, former capitalist colonies which comprise the Third World. The obliteration of the coolies and the subsequent removal by emigration of virtually every second person born in Ireland made it possible for those remaining in the country to secure living standards, values and aspirations approximating to those of the West, while Ireland continued to have the undeveloping economy of a former capitalist colony. For forty years government deficit financing made it possible for rather more people to secure those standards. But now, after forty years of dependence on deficit financing, the entire rickety socio-economic structure of a society with the standards of the West and a Third World economy has become as vulnerable as was Irish society after sixty years of George III and complete dependence on the exotic potato. Then markets changed and the potatoes failed. Now the imminent dangers are the tightening of the escape valve of emigration and the exhaustion of the state's credit.

An historic period, that of factory capitalist colonialism, has ended; and with it the easy absorption of that half of the Irish made surplus by the institutional framework. The change in the external situation, which makes it no longer so easy for the Irish to get abroad the jobs they have always been denied at home, parallels that other change in external conditions which occurred after the Napoleonic Wars. Both changes threw up great surpluses of people. In the earlier period, those surplus people were forced to rely on the fickle and exotic potato. Now the surplus people are forced into dependence on the state's credit with fickle foreign bankers. The state's credit, like the potato in the 1840s, becomes more vulnerable and less reliable the longer and more completely it is relied on. As disease organisms and the disease resistance of the potato varieties grown in the early 19th century declined, so now the weight of service charges on existing debt grows and the ability of a weakened economy to survive without credit declines.

It is important to stress that just as no society was as dependent on the potato or as vulnerable to its failure as Ireland was in the period 1820-1850, now no economy is as dependent on state credit as the Irish one is. Ireland's public debt relative to GNP:

  a) is the largest in the world: public debt equalled 160% of
     GNP in 1987;
  b) is the most costly to service in the world: interest on the
     public debt in 1986 was the equivalent of 14% of GNP;
                          and
  c) is the most rapidly growing in the world: it grew by the
     equivalent of 19% of GNP in 1986.

Sixty-five years on, the Irish economy is back again to a position similar to that of 1922, immediately after the break with Britain. A number of expedients have been tried and found to yield short-term benefit but longer term aggravation of the original weakness. Protection gave jobs in the 1930s; but it was no longer tenable in the 1950s, by which time it had done irreparable harm to older, non-protected industries. Deficit financing, particularly with the Whitaker strategem built in, made all things possible, including a public debt in 1987 equivalent to 160% of GNP. Servicing that debt now compounds all the original structural weaknesses that were in the capitalist colonial economy of 1922.

Joining the EEC seemed, in 1972, the answer to 50 years of failed self-government. Fifteen years of membership of a Community comprising all the former capitalist colonial powers has done nothing to alleviate, but much to aggravate,

66

the problems of the former colony. This happened also with the earlier Union with Britain, which brought untold hardship on the Irish masses, while, as intended, securing the position of the elites who engineered the Union. The new Union likewise has resulted in wholesale loss of jobs, a quadrupling of unemployment and an increasingly extreme dependence on subsidies from, and credit through, the EEC.

The Irish economy is now substantially weaker than it was in 1922. Apart from the fact that it is the only country in the world where the number of people at work is less – 20% less – than it was then, its economy is now much less competitive and much more dependent. Ireland in 1922 had an agriculture which competed on foreign markets, if not brilliantly at least without subsidies. Now according to a recent study by the OECD, of every £100 Irish farmers put in their pockets, £93 has come either from EEC taxpayers in the form of subsidies, or from EEC consumers in the form of unnecessarily high food prices. The 133,000 workers in Irish manufacturing industry in 1922 may not have earned a lot, but they produced traded goods for the home market, which Irish manufacturing industry no longer does. Only goods that are little traded internationally, like Irish newspapers, bread and mineral waters, are now produced for the home market. Irish manufacturing industry in 1922 was locally owned and exported without benefit of subsidy or tax relief. Now all the additional jobs in manufacturing industry (up from 133,000 to 193,000) are in export industries that are foreign-owned and are located in Ireland because of subsidies and tax holidays. Payment of the subsidies and the tax holidays to the foreign owners of Irish export industry is made possible by public sector borrowing. The state acquires, through foreign borrowing, the money which the foreign entrepreneurs repatriate as capital amortization and profit. The country's surviving jobs are thus largely dependent on the EEC's continuing to pay unnecessarily high prices for food; and on foreign creditors continuing to lend to an Irish state that now has, relative to GNP, the largest debt in the world.

It is true, of course, that the half of the Irish who, since independence, have managed to get jobs at home have real incomes that are much higher than formerly. But that is no new thing. Broadly speaking, the rate of improvement in Irish incomes and the rate of decline in the number able to get those incomes have been the same in the seventy years since 1916 as they were in the seventy years before 1916. Independence has made no difference to the rate of undevelopment of Ireland any more than it has in any other former capitalist colony.

Sixty-five years on, the expedients are exhausted. Establishment orthodoxy now, as in 1922, is free trade, frugal government and balanced budgets. But now the economy is structurally much weaker; emigration is less easy; the state's credit is virtually exhausted. There is a public debt which, relative to GNP, is the largest and most expensive to service in the world.

There is no light at the end of this tunnel. The unbroken record of undevelopment in all former capitalist colonies is that the road the nation now follows ends in collapse and chaos. The experience of 65 years of self-government points to the same ending. But that is of less consequence to the poweraholic establishment than that they should remain in charge. Hence their insistence that there is no alternative to the present course though it must end in disaster.

The uniqueness of the Irish situation and the termination of the conditions which have created that uniqueness give hope that Ireland may unprecedentedly transform capitalist colonial undevelopment into development. The reasonably well-nourished, well-educated casualties of Ireland's corrupt, inequitable and inefficient socio-economic order can no longer easily escape. Moreover, with the near exhaustion of the State's credit, the privileges created by that order will be withdrawn from many of those who have hitherto shared them. Unlike that earlier crisis in the 1840s, there is now no army of occupation to maintain an imposed socio-economic order which, for almost two centuries, has denied a livelihood to half the people. These fundamental changes create political conditions favourable to an unprecedented transformation of capitalist colonial undevelopment into development.

From Undevelopment to Development

It is not difficult to identify the nature of the change that is necessary to transform Irish undevelopment into development. That change is determined by the character of capitalist colonial undevelopment and the mechanism of its implementation, as analyzed here. It involves essentially eliminating capitalist colonial privilege and its associated disabilities which are maintained by a state that is the direct descendant of and heir to England's Dublin Castle rule in Ireland. Producers are charged too little for land and capital and too much for labour. It is necessary to change this pattern of costs so that producers pay more for land and capital and less for labour. This can easily and effectively be done by taxing the resources that are too cheap (land and capital/savings) and by detaxing the resource that is too dear (labour). The cost of resources to producers can in this way be made to reflect their economic value rather than to reflect inherited capital colonial privilege.

All taxes should be removed from labour (i.e. PAYE, PRSI) and the things that labour buys (VAT). Tax revenue from land and from the financial system (including banks, insurance companies and building societies) should be maximized. In addition, in order to save revenue and to preclude further borrowing by corrupt and corrupting politicians, the public debt should be repudiated. These fiscal changes are likely to be self-financing. To the extent that they are not, retrospective taxation of the persons most responsible and of those who have profited most from the retention for 65 years of a system of capitalist colonial privilege and associated disability could be used to make good any shortfall.

The proposed fiscal changes would transform Ireland's undeveloping economy into a developing one. Given that transformation, it would be feasible to reappraise critically the Irish state. The state is the enemy of the nation and has been the cause of its undevelopment. But even as the nation has been undeveloped by the state's actions, the people have looked more and more to the state to remedy the situation. The analogy of the horse with its reins entangled in its harness, backing away and in doing so being forced to back further, seems again relevant. Once the reins are severed, in this case by the proposed fiscal changes, the nation might look critically at its enemy the state.

The suggested fiscal changes are likely to be self-financing. The resources foregone by abolishing PAYE, PRSI, VAT and public sector borrowing can be recouped from taxes on land and the financial system and by savings in servicing the public debt. This will leave some £6,500 million of the nation's resources in the public exchequer. It would be possible for the state to use those resources as at present. An alternative democratic use for them would be to distribute them equally to every member of the nation; or rather to every person on the voters' register and resident in Ireland. That would make possible the payment of what might be called a national dividend of some £2,700 per annum to all the 2.4 million persons on the voters' register. Given the proposed abolition of VAT, that would be equivalent to in excess of £3,000/ annum in terms of 1987 prices. If allowance is made for the further price reductions that would be made possible by the elimination of PAYE and PRSI, the suggested national dividend could be worth £4,000 per annum, or more, in 1987 prices.

The alternatives mentioned, that of the state continuing at its present scale, with no national dividend; and that of the level of the state's activities being reduced to zero with a national dividend equivalent to around £80 per week at 1987 prices, are the extremes of a spectrum. Between these two extremes lie a continuum of combinations of more or less state activity and correspondingly less or more national dividend. It is quite feasible to design a system which would allow every citizen regularly to vote for the preferred combination of state expenditure and national dividend and from the votes cast to arrive at the combination of state expenditure and national dividend which, from time to time, most closely reflected the national will.

In such a situation it can be said, in general, that poor people with little money will prefer to maximize the national dividend and correspondingly to minimize the state. On the other hand, wealthy people with much money will prefer to preserve the state, especially in its role of protector of their wealth.

These are the matters I have attempted to deal with and to set out in *Ireland in Crisis: A Study in Capitalist Colonialism Undevelopment,* which was published in 1986. But to analyze, to explain, to propose, to write books is insufficient. It is incumbent on all Irish people to do now whatever they can to avert the disasters that threaten the country and the nation. That is why I found myself challenging the Single European Act.

CHAPTER 4

The Approaching SEA

Life is a landscape littered with windmills. To get by, it is important to recognize those at which one should not tilt. The insights I acquired into the economics of Irish farming, later into the Irish economy, and later again into the undeveloping economies of Ireland and the Third World, were, I believed, important. To develop and present these effectively was more than enough challenge for my limited personal resources. That, plus a fair measure of natural indolence, had caused me to husband scarce resources and to tilt rarely at windmills. Ireland's proposed membership of the European Economic Community, when it became a political issue in 1969, was not however a matter from which one could reasonably seek to refrain in order better to pursue superior long-term objectives. Regard for those long term objectives appeared on that occasion to require departing temporarily from the study of the undevelopment of Ireland and of the former capitalist colonies; and to make a public stand on the issue of Irish membership of the EEC.

Battles Long Ago

"Don't you know there's a war on" was the standard rejoinder 45 years ago to the standard cribs made by standardly unhappy people. In the years before the Second World War and for some years after, the standard rejoinder in Ireland had been: "What can you expect after six hundred years of English rule?" At least now, 60 years plus after the ending of that rule, less is heard of that particular excuse; though occasionally, and particularly from Dr. Garret FitzGerald, one does hear reference to its updated, electronic age counterpart, "British neo-colonialism", as the cause of Ireland's woes.

"British neo-colonialism", particularly as manifested by a not unreasonable concern to buy their imports, including food, as cheaply as possible, was – and indeed for some continues to be – the chief source of the problems of Irish agriculture. Were it not for this evil, and seemingly particularly British, preoccupation with cheap food – hardly less evil than their contraceptives, divorce and free love – Irish agriculture would boom and the country would flow with milk and honey. Joining the EEC was seen as the means of escaping from this cruel yoke of "British neo-colonialism". It was seen particularly as a means of getting much higher prices for Irish farmers and simultaneously of relieving the exchequer of the cost of subsidising agricultural exports. For butter alone, that cost in 1970 was £30 millions or 2% of current GNP. In terms of present prices and GNP, it was the equivalent of £330 millions.

The in-term "marketing", or indeed agricultural prices, had never seemed to me, at least since the early 1950s when I commenced figuring these matters out for myself, as anything other than catch-cries to excuse palpable failure in organizing production. They were part of the game of blaming others, particularly the Brits, for our problems. This is an understandable activity and an innocuous one unless carried too far, as I first perceived it to be in Ireland and have subsequently perceived it to be in every former capitalist colony I have known. The trouble is that, while blaming the Brits in our case, the North American Gringos in the case of Latin America, the Whites in the case of Africa and so on, may help salve pride wounded by failure, it distracts from the fact that we are all big, grown-up people now; we are all politically independent and therefore responsible for our own destinies. Blaming others for our problems is not a substitute for action to resolve those problems.

The inefficiencies of Irish farming and the associated poor showing of the Irish economy owed nothing to the low prices available on export markets. They owed everything to the high cost of inputs, other than land, into Irish farming, and to the associated cause of the low cost of holding land. These problems we had acquired in 1922 as part of the capitalist colonial heritage; but successive Irish governments had consistently made them worse. The final, clinching action was the abolition of the last remnant of a land tax in the 1987 Budget.

The problem was, and is, policies, not prices. EEC membership in 1972 was about prices. Insofar as policy was concerned, there was the Common Agricultural Policy or CAP, designed for the circumstances of the former capitalist colonial powers Germany, France, Italy, Belgium and the Netherlands, the original six members of the EEC, which Britain, Denmark, Norway and Ireland now proposed to join. Ireland's application for EEC membership was a case of the propagandist being misled by his own propaganda. It was a case of our not simply indulging in the favourite pastime of Brit-bashing, but of proceeding to escape from the entirely imaginary yoke of British neo-colonialism by joining the EEC.

The gilt had not yet, in the early 1970s, worn off the Whitakerian miracle. This was based on borrowing to subsidise exports and so to postpone the balance of payments deficit and loss of foreign exchange reserves which are the inevitable consequence of sustained public sector deficit financing. The economy was growing more rapidly than ever before and people were talking about "an economic take-off". They were overlooking the great and growing weight of public debt, which was guaranteed to anchor any economy firmly in a morass of failure once the hot air from the state's credit ran out. In this euphoria, it was possible for establishment economists to write and to speak facilely of protected Irish manufacturing industry switching from the protected home market to the vast EEC market, and to be believed.

The dross beneath "the Irish economic miracle" was not difficult to perceive for anyone not blinded by self-interest and concern for career advancement or private fortune. The king was indeed starkers. The Irish economy in 1972 was, in critical matters, substantially weaker and less competitive than it had been in 1922. Agriculture was hopelessly dependent on subsidies financed by state borrowing.

74

Virtually all local manufacturing industry was dependent on protection; or else it was of the fly-by-night, IDA-backed enclave type, here for the grants, subsidies and tax-holidays and gone with the first wisp of recession. The time-bomb of public debt was ticking louder by the minute. And the acid test was that there were 165,000, or 14%, fewer people at work in 1972 than in 1922.

Everyone on the establishment bandwagon was not, of course, blind to the major weaknesses of the Irish economy. For many, joining the EEC was the only way of escaping the problems confronting the country. Having experienced fifty years of independence and having found that painting the red letter-boxes green had achieved nothing, these were prepared for Ireland to abdicate from the responsibilities of sovereignty and to throw in its lot once more, as with the Act of Union in 1800, with a metropolitan power.

But this advocacy of a return by the errant capitalist colonial child to the metropolitan mama's fold was based on an inadequate and incorrect understanding of capitalist colonial undevelopment. That undevelopment stemmed initially from a wrong ordering superimposed for metropolitan profit on Irish society. It has, subsequent to independence, been maintained in Ireland and in every former capitalist colony, for the benefit of the indigenous interests created by capitalist colonialism. Surrendering a sovereignty that has not been used in Ireland, or in any other former capitalist colony, for the purpose of transforming a bad social order into a good one, may be akin to removing pearls from swine; but what was to replace the pearls of sovereignty was the already tried swill of dependence. Yet while there was life there was hope that a swinish nature might yet give way to a rational humanity, capable of appreciating the virtually limitless potential of the sovereign capacity to order the affairs of a nation. On the record of Ireland or any other former capitalist colony, there was nothing to lose by surrendering a sovereignty that had achieved nothing. There was loss only if sovereignty was valued for its potential rather than its actuality.

Abandoning a failed independence for a return to dependence would result in a transfer from the metropolitan core to the colonial periphery. Similar transfers had occurred from Britain to Ireland, especially during the final decades of Irish capital colonialism; and continue between Britain and Northern Ireland. The pre-1922 transfer from Britain to Ireland, or the present one to Northern Ireland, though they may have slowed it, had not reversed economic undevelopment and its attendant social evils. Even if those transfers were on a substantially greater scale from the metropolitan EEC to the Irish periphery, this throwing of money at a problem would not undo the underlying cause of an inappropriate, imposed social order. It was like offering a crutch to a person crippled with ill-fitting boots.

Indeed, because of what I called "the paradox of property" the resources expected from the EEC were likely themselves to do harm rather than good. The principal benefit, expected higher EEC farm prices, would raise the value of Irish land and to that extent would aggravate all the problems of property in Irish land, which I perceived to be the very fountain-head of Irish economic undevelopment. As land values appreciated relative to general incomes, which by 1978 they had done eightfold since the state's foundation, the retained possession of land by incompetent persons became easier and more attractive. Simultaneously, the acquisition of land by competent, landless, resourceless young people, who could best use it, became even more unlikely. Agricultural output as a result would not increase.

Though higher farm prices would not raise agricultural output, they would raise living costs and therefore production costs in all sectors. This was particularly important for indigenous Irish manufacturing which, under EEC rules, was simultaneously to be exposed to greater competition from imports as Irish industrial protection was removed. It was all very well for permanently, pensionably and lucratively employed academics to preach from their ivory towers of the need to shift resources from producing for a declining domestic market to producing for an expanding EEC market. Their preaching would have carried more conviction had they been able to quote even one case of manufacturing industry expanding into exports while the domestic market was being lost. The example of 140 former capitalist colonies suggests that when the domestic market is destroyed, the resources which have produced for it are transferred not to export industries, but to the scrapheap.

It was clear to me that EEC membership would not at all transform Irish economic undevelopment into development. It would probably expedite the undevelopment process as union with Britain did in 1800. Then the collapse of an utterly inappropriate social order, which would certainly have otherwise ensued during the early crisis decades of the 19th century, was prevented by the application of British military and police force to a malnourished and illiterate population. Now the transfer of resources, coupled with continuing emigration, would act to assuage the forces of social disintegration and help to preserve, possibly indefinitely, a fundamentally inappropriate social order. Ireland, once the Achilles' heel of the British Empire, would become the running sore of Europe, its festering sustained by constant feeding by the metropolitan centre.

Considerations of this nature suggested the desirability of deviating from the main task, of studying and attempting to explain the process of capitalist undevelopment, in order to participate in the Common Market Defence Campaign (CMDC) to block Irish entry into the EEC. There was no expectation that the walls of the establishment would collapse; the most to be hoped for was that a statement of dissent and the reasons for that dissent would be registered. That was done.

On that occasion I came into contact for the first time with people who were involved one way or another with national, as distinct from vocational, politics. At various times I had been the first honorary secretary of Kilkenny Young Farmers Club (though as pointed out at the time, there are no young farmers or small rats, only "old" farmers and "big" rats) which was subsequently to be transmogrified into Macra na Feirme, the National Farmers' Association and now the Irish Farmers' Association. I had been secretary of the County Kilkenny branch of the Beet Growers Association; a member of the National Council of the Irish Creamery Milk Suppliers' Association; and an economic consultant to that organisation and to the Irish National Land League, so I knew a little of farm politics and politicians. But the CMDC was my first contact with persons aiming through political action for something other than a few pence more on the price of milk or a few bob a barrel more for wheat.

Out of the Limelight

The CMDC ended on 10 May 1972, with 1,042,000 out of a total poll of 1,264,000 voting to have the Constitution amended so as to permit Ireland's entry to the EEC. Only 212,000, or 17% of those who voted, shared my view that Ireland should remain outside the EEC. Occasionally I wondered if the time and effort spent persuading more people to vote against EEC membership were worthwhile. Marginally it seems yes. One's position was publicly stated. But once the 1972 EEC Referendum was out of the way, there was little further distraction from what I perceived as my main task of analysing and describing the process of capitalist colonial undevelopment. The all too meagre results of that work were the two books to which I have already referred.

Apart from my natural indolence, there was no issue sufficiently compelling to distract me as the CMDC had been. Some of those engaged in the CMDC had proceeded to form the Irish Sovereignty Movement. While retaining a warm regard for these former fellow campaigners, I found myself out of sympathy with what they seemed to regard as the major issues of the day. While maintaining an interest in EEC matters, they also became involved with "the National issue" (or Northern Ireland), the Bomb, and South African Apartheid. For me unquestionably the main issue, the issue in comparison with which everything else seemed at best insignificant and at worst a distracting red herring, was the failure of half the Irish for almost two centuries to get a livelihood in Ireland, parallelled by the widening, deepening poverty of the masses of the Third World; and which now in Ireland was manifesting itself increasingly in mass unemployment.

Twenty-six Counties had seceded from the UK, and in doing so had partitioned themselves off from the predominantly Protestant part of the island which refused to secede. The secessionists were right to secede; but in seceding they incurred the obligation to create in the Twenty-six Counties a society worthy of the Irish nation. Had they done so, then the rest of Ireland would probably have followed the Twenty-six Counties. Or if they did not, it would have been a matter of little or no consequence.

The denial of a livelihood to half the people of the Twenty-six Counties, under independence no less than under British government, ruled out any possibility that the Protestants of Northern Ireland would throw in their lot with the Catholics of the South. Protestant privilege had enabled a much larger proportion of Protestants than of Catholics to get a livelihood in Ireland so that the proportion of Protestants in the island's workforce had increased from around 20% in 1841 to nearly 30% in 1971. Meanwhile, as all incomes in Ireland rose, Catholic resentment at Protestant privilege in Northern Ireland firmed and became more effective. It was quite irresponsible, under the circumstances, for people in the Twenty-six Counties to encourage that resentment, which could only result in increasingly bitter competition for jobs between Catholics and Protestants in an Ireland where only half the population has been able for 160 years to get a livelihood. Meddling in Northern Ireland matters was particularly irresponsible for people living in the South, where most of the loss of livelihood had incurred and where alone effective action could be taken to end the denial of a livelihood to so many which fundamentally is the cause of mayhem in Northern Ireland.

The possibility of nuclear conflagration was another preoccupation of the ISM, as indeed it is of other Irish non-party political organizations. This is an inherent part of those Western values and aspirations which Ireland shares with the Western World and which are quite out of keeping with the undeveloping Irish economy of a former capitalist colony. In no other former capitalist colony have I witnessed the preoccupation with a hypothetical nuclear conflagration which obtains among the affluent and secure peoples of the West. The peoples of the Third World are too preoccupied with the pressing immediate problems of their poverty to be able to indulge in concern about hypothetical future problems. To the barely conceivable extent that the starving people of Africa might be able to spare a moment for the idea of nuclear conflagration, they would as likely as not, welcome it as a release from their present misery. In a small country where half the people are denied a livelihood and can no longer easily emigrate, it seems reasonable to leave the matter of nuclear world conflagration to others in the non-capitalist-colonized, developing world who, for the most part, have made the bombs.

Apartheid was another concern of the ISM and similar groups which engaged much public attention in the relatively affluent 1970s and early 1980s. The cleavage between White and Black in South Africa is a much worse abomination than that between Protestant and Catholic in Northern Ireland. It is worse because it is on a greater scale, the population of South Africa being 22 million compared to Northern Ireland's 1.5 million. It is worse because South African apartheid is imposed more rigorously than the Protestant/Catholic divide is in Northern Ireland. It is, for example, much less conceivable that a black resident of the Soweto district would move to the Killarney district of Johannesburg than that a Catholic resident of the Falls Road would move to the Shankill Road in Belfast. The White/Black divide in South Africa is also worse than the Protestant/Catholic divide in Ireland because in South Africa there is no external power willing to pour in resources to ameliorate the conflict as Britain does in Northern Ireland. Understandably, the murders and maimings stemming from apartheid are on a vaster scale than those arising from the Protestant/Catholic struggle in Northern Ireland.

There is, despite the differences, a fundamental identity in the White/Black struggle in South Africa and the Protestant/ Catholic struggle in the North. In both cases settlers from metropolitan countries, having forced out indigenous crop growers, have incorporated their own sweat and blood into the land. In both cases, as part of the worldwide process of ending capitalist colonialism, the decendants of the ousted indigenes are struggling to regain an equal place in the sun with the conquerors. That struggle is of a life and death, murderous nature principally because it takes place within the context of capitalist colonial undevelopment. Whites in South Africa cling to the privileges that have made for them an island of prosperity in a sea of Black economic chaos throughout the rest of Africa, just as the Protestants of Northern Ireland cling to the privileges that have enabled a higher proportion of them to secure a livelihood in this island.

It is as unthinkable that the Whites of South Africa can be bludgeoned into abandoning their privileges as it is that the Protestants of Northern Ireland can be forced to do likewise. And even if the Whites of South Africa and the Protestants of Northern Ireland were so bludgeoned, all that would be achieved would be an extension of the economic chaos of the rest of Africa to its southern tip; and of the economic failure of the rest of Ireland to its north-eastern tip. The way to end racial strife in South Africa, as to end sectarian strife in Northern Ireland, is to end the murderous struggle for a livelihood which is characteristic of the undeveloping economies of all former capitalist colonies. If Black Africa was not quite such an economic hell, the South African Whites would not resist so firmly encroachments on their privileges and the Blacks would not be driven so desperately to attempt those encroachments. If Southern Ireland ended both emigration and unemployment, Protestants and Catholics would cease to murder one another in competition for jobs in Northern Ireland. There was nothing I could directly do to bring about such a situation in Africa; but by pursuing the work of analysing and explaining economic undevelopment in Ireland, I might be able to do something constructive towards removing the cause of sectarian strife in Northern Ireland. If a precedent were created, by transforming Irish undevelopment into development, then it might be repeated in Africa, making racial strife as irrelevant in South Africa as sectarian strife would be in Northern Ireland. This line of reasoning pointed clearly to sticking to the main task and keeping my nose out of other people's business where one was more likely to do harm than good.

Considerations of this nature made it easy to move off the stage of public affairs when the joining-the-EEC show ended with the 1972 Referendum. In particular, I ceased to be "an EEC-watcher", paying no more attention to the goings-on in Brussels than to any other issues that impinged on public life. It was the easier to remain aloof from the Euro-shenanigans because of the great disillusionment about the EEC that had taken place. By the 1980s, the EEC itself was patently running out of steam; and the great hopes and expectations of what it would do for Ireland had been disappointed. Irish farming, for which so much had been expected, was in a worse mess than ever, with a third fewer people getting a livelihood from it than before Ireland joined the EEC. Milk and sugarbeet were on quota, and it was only a matter of time before the other main products, beef and cereals, were also put on quota or the whole Common Agricultural Policy was wound up. The overall Irish economy had deteriorated far more than I had expected, notwithstanding the receipt of much greater than anticipated transfers from outside in the form of EEC agricultural subsidies and foreign credits. Clearly the centre of decision-taking for Ireland had not shifted from Dublin to Brussels. If the basic task of transforming capitalist colonial undevelopment into development was to be accomplished, the Irish and the Irish alone could do it.

Moreover, whatever had been the original intention of the Treaty of Rome, the EEC had evolved along lines that made Irish membership of that body increasingly incongruous. The EEC had become virtually an exclusive club of former capitalist colonial powers, banded together now to retain, maybe even to recover, something of their vanished glory and dominance in the world. The original EEC members had been joined in 1972 by two other former capitalist colonial powers, Britain and Denmark; and by Ireland, Europe's only former capitalist colony. The Norwegian people had voted to remain aloof. In 1981, Greece joined the EEC; finally the two original capitalist colonial powers, Spain and Portugal joined in 1986. The list of former imperial powers was now complete. Apart from Ireland, Europe's only former capitalist colony, and Greece, whose people sought to escape military dictatorship, none of the other European countries which have not been imperial powers has agreed to join the EEC.

Increased Dependence

My analysis of Ireland's problems, *Ireland in Crisis: A Study in Capitalist Colonial Undevelopment,* was published in May 1986. Despite the hassle of getting a book published and despite my deliberate aloofness from EEC affairs, it was not possible to ignore the Single European Act (SEA) which in February of that year the Heads of Government of the member states of the EEC had undertaken to have ratified by the end of the year. The necessary legislation was introduced to Dail Eireann in September 1986.

The SEA is an attempt to get an increasingly unwieldy and uninspiring EEC show "back on the road", as they say. The resurgence from the ashes of the Second World War of the original six Common Market countries, every one of which had experienced invasion and defeat between 1939 and 1945, was miraculous. When Britain, Denmark and Ireland joined the EEC in 1972, the six original member countries had experienced 27 years of continuous, rapid economic growth in a manner unparalleled in history. That growth had gone far to restore Europe's old economic and political dominance in the world. It had restored European confidence, shattered by defeat at the hands of the two non European powers, the USA and the USSR, and it had given ground for hope that, in Europe at least, the age old struggle against want could be won.

But from 1972 to 1986 progress was much slower in the enlarged EEC. The Community appeared increasingly to be engulfed in a sea of trouble. The principal currents in that sea were massive, growing unemployment; equally massive and growing agricultural surpluses; and the threat of relegation by the new world powers, the USA, the USSR and Japan. The former confidence and optimism generated by the successful recovery from wartime destruction had been replaced by a defensiveness which reflected the relative failure of the more recent period. This important change in mood is captured by a comparison of the preambles of the original Treaty of Rome, establishing the EEC, and that of the SEA. Where, for example, the preamble to the Treaty of Rome is "RESOLVED by thus pooling their resources to preserve and strengthen peace and liberty, and calling upon the other peoples of Europe who share their ideal to join in these efforts ... etc."; the preamble to the SEA reads: "AWARE of the responsibility incumbent upon Europe to aim at speaking ever increasingly with one voice and to act with consistency and solidarity in order more effectively to protect its common interests and independence ... etc."

That new defensiveness implicit in the SEA is made explicit in the Irish Government's Blue Book *The Single European Act: An Explanatory Guide:* "In recent years the Community has failed to keep pace with the United States and Japan in terms of economic growth, job creation and the development of advanced technology". Or again: "It is essential that the Community be fully equipped to compete effectively in the area of research and high technology where it has lost considerable ground to the United States and Japan in recent years".

With *Ireland in Crisis* published, it was possible to take a closer look at the SEA. I was particularly concerned about the economic implications, given that the purpose of the Treaty was, as explained subsequently by Commissioner Peter Sutherland: "to ensure that the wider Community interest prevails". The wider interest of a Community of all the world's former imperial powers virtually by definition involved damage to Ireland, Europe's only former capitalist colony. It was important to discover how the SEA would work for the "wider Community interest" and to the detriment of Ireland. Given the obscure character of the SEA, that was not easy.

The first point to note was that the requirement of unanimity in the EEC Council of Ministers of the EEC for decisions pertaining to a range of important issues was to be greatly circumscribed. The unanimity requirement specified in the Treaty of Rome, and confirmed by the Treaty of Accession of Ireland to the EEC, was a constitutional safeguard for Irish interests when these conflicted with "the wider Community interest" of the world's former imperial powers. It was quite a different matter from the better known, so-called "veto", or "Luxembourg compromise", exercised rarely when vital national interests are deemed to be involved. This "veto" was used only once by Ireland, in 1985, to delay a proposed cut in the amount of milk for which Irish farmers would receive a high guaranteed price. The veto inherent in a unanimity requirement operated regularly in the proceedings of the Council of Ministers, the EEC's equivalent to the cabinet of a national government. One of the consequences of adopting majority voting would be to expedite the implementation of several hundred pieces of legislation which had already been proposed by the Commission of the EEC and which are listed in the Cockfield report, *Completing the Internal Market.*

The implications of the SEA for monetary and banking policy were less obvious but more serious. An apparently innocuous Article 20 deals in general terms with "cooperation in economic and monetary policy". Teeth are given to this aspiration by a series of amendments hidden away in the text of the SEA, the significance of which becomes manifest only after diligent search. The effect of these amendments is to remove the unanimity requirement specified in the Treaty of Rome and in the Treaty of Accession "on measures concerned with the protection of savings, in particular the granting of credit and the exercise of the banking profession". These matters would now pass out of the control of the Government of Ireland, which relative to its GNP has the largest public debt in the world, and into the control of a qualified majority of ministers representing states which are among the major creditor countries in the world.

Creditors in Ireland might welcome the prospect of competition from foreign banks, building societies and insurance companies in the hitherto protected Irish market for these services. But the broader implications would be to sweep away all those impediments by which the Irish Central Bank now tries to stem the outflow of funds from Ireland. Not only the new banks entering Ireland, but those already established there, would be free to hold their assets wherever they wished. They could no longer be required, as Irish banks now are, to hold 25% of their deposits in depreciating Irish government securities. Likewise insurance companies and building societies, both Irish and foreign, would be free to move their funds where they wished. They could no longer be forced to hold them in Ireland where they are subject to the increasingly obvious danger of devaluation of the currency. The SEA removes the remaining power of Irish governments to curb the outflow of Irish savings. Irish savers will be able to invest abroad directly, instead of as now indirectly through the purchase of the shares of Irish companies like Smurfits, Independent Newspapers, MacInerney, Cement Roadstone, Crean and Allied Irish Banks. These companies have effectively ceased to invest in Ireland and are concentrating their investment abroad. In other words the SEA, as well as expediting the flow of goods, would also expedite the flow of savings; and for Ireland as a heavily indebted, undeveloping former capitalist colony, that flow of funds would be one way only – outwards.

Establishment proponents of the EEC pointed to the overwhelming importance of exports in the Irish economy. These, at the equivalent of nearly 60% of GNP, were relatively greater than in any other EEC country; or indeed in any of the advanced economies which comprise the OECD. They contended that removing the remaining barriers to the free flow of trade was therefore particularly important for Ireland. But this is a one-sided, unbalanced view of the matter.

William Petty, in the 17th century, proposed turning Ireland into a cattlewalk, producing nothing but pastoral products for export. Had other interests not intervened to thwart this plan, and incidentally to save the Irish nation from extinction, Ireland would have ended with exports amounting to nearly 100% of GNP, with everything other than pastoral products being imported. Irish exports are so large relative to GNP not because exports are large, but because Irish GNP is small. And Irish GNP is small largely because so much Irish industry has been wiped out by the imports that have been facilitated by freeing trade. There is not the slightest doubt about the trade consequences of the further freeing of trade aimed at by the SEA. While there may be some short-term increase in exports from the undeveloping, peripheral former capitalist colony of Ireland to the developing core, former imperial powers of the EEC, there will be an even greater increase in imports, particularly now of services; and Ireland will move a step further towards Petty's vision of a sparsely inhabited cattlewalk exporting pastoral products only.

How could it be otherwise? Who under free trade conditions and with common policies would wish to locate an industry in the Irish periphery if there was the alternative of locating at the core? To achieve a similar scale and therefore similar cost of production, an Irish producer would have to export perhaps 95% of output, while the core producer could serve a small

Irish market by exporting a few per cent of an output, most of which would be sold locally in the large core market. Only very exceptional local attractions, or a heroic commitment to an Irish location regardless of costs, could induce an entrepreneur to incur the great additional expense either of small scale production for a local Irish market, or of shipping the bulk of output across what has been described as the most costly stretch of water in the world – that separating Ireland from its EEC partners.

The SEA was thus another important milestone on the path towards Irish economic undevelopment. It marked yet another stage in the growing dependence of the former capitalist colony on the former imperial powers. The proponents of the SEA might mention, with tongue in cheek, the opportunities for greater exports; but the grants and loans from the EEC, on which the economy has now become utterly dependent, are incontrovertibly real. Maintaining for a little while longer the existing socio-economic order depends critically in the first place on the £1 billion per year which Ireland receives in grants from the EEC; and in the second place on the further £1 billion which Ireland borrows annually from abroad and is able to do so in large measure because of its EEC membership. Not surprisingly, membership of the EEC and everything that is conducive to securing that is part of the political establishment's consensus.

There was another aspect of the SEA which was of concern, given Ireland's position as an undeveloping former capitalist colony in a Community of former imperial powers. While holding no brief for de Valera or the Fianna Fail party which he founded, I did see much merit in de Valera's Constitution. It is a jealous Constitution, in the sense that it recognises that political power emanates from the people. As the preamble to the Constitution puts it: "We, the people of Eire ... hereby adopt, enact and give to ourselves this Constitution". That is a far cry from the English concept of "the sovereignty of the crown in Parliament". The Constitution is redolent of Ireland's history of government by a metropolitan power for the purpose of exploiting the people of the colony for the profit of the metropolis. The Constitution is a profoundly democratic document which articulates the Irish people's well-grounded

87

suspicion of government and their traditional, well-justified posture of being "agin the government".

The Irish constitutional position, reflecting the nation's history, is very different not only from Britain's, but from that of the other EEC members. There is in Ireland an assumption of the corruption, or the original sin, of government, while in the other countries there is an assumption of constitutionality and legitimacy in government. The Irish position is akin to that of the USA, where there was also a struggle to throw off a tyrannical colonial government. Perhaps more to the point, the Irish position is akin to that of most former capitalist colonies, which, like Ireland, have noble constitutions with noble aspirations. The trouble in these other former capitalist colonies is that their constitutions are not worth the paper on which they are written. It is one thing to have a fine constitution; it is quite another matter to implement it, as the constitutions of the USA and Ireland have been implemented.

Constitutional government, or the rule of law, is a fine and rare thing. It is a distinctively European phenomenon. In Europe alone did it evolve spontaneously, slowly, hesitantly and with many backward slips. The circumstances unique to Europe which brought it about I have endeavoured to treat of elsewhere. Those circumstances are of a socio-economic character. They are not in any sense racial. The white skins of Europeans do not in any way fit them especially well for constitutional government or the rule of law. That this is so is borne out by the dictatorial governments that normally rule in the southern cone of South America, although the populations of Argentina and Chile are overwhelmingly of Caucasian origin. And, of course, Russian autocracy has always been far removed from the rule of law

Promulgation of a constitution does not ensure constitutional government. Constitutional government can emerge and survive only under specific and rare socio-economic conditions. The USA was fortunate in sharing with Europe the socio-economic conditions that have made constitutional government, as well as economic development, possible. Ireland, alone of the former capitalist colonies, has also experienced the socio-economic conditions essential for constitutional government. But in Ireland's case, those socio-economic conditions which have also given Ireland the living standards and aspirations of the West, have been created by the emigration of the less contented half of six generations. Without that emigration, it is as certain as anything can be in an uncertain world that though Ireland might and probably would have given itself a noble constitution, that constitution would have remained a dead letter. The noble constitutions, like the shelves full of ambitious economic plans of the unfortunate former capitalist colonies which comprise the Third World, are merely a quaint, mocking glimpse of a different world. They are without relevance to a reality where poverty and hopelessness are endemic, where life is cheap and where the will of the dictator of the moment is law.

Law in Ireland, as in the USA, has been given to the people by the people. And that law is directed especially at controlling government which, through centuries of colonialism, has been the agent for the exploition of the people for the profit and in the interests of the metropolitan power. So far law, in the form of de Valera's Constitution, has been eminently successful in controlling government in Ireland. Although the constitution will not prevail if the forthcoming crisis is not successfully resolved, it is of the utmost importance to preserve it as a tripwire against the encroachments of the state, which in every other former capitalist colony has made a mockery of constitutional government.

The constitutional aspects of the SEA are complex, possibly made deliberately so in order to discourage a wider public, and possibly critical, attention. Briefly, from the viewpoint of the Irish Constitution, there are two distinct parts of the SEA. One deals with amending and expanding existing legislation covered in the Treaty of Rome, the Irish Treaty of Accession to the EEC and other treaties. That part of the SEA has been referred to as Titles I and II. The other part of the SEA purports to give the EEC new responsibilities and powers not covered in the Treaty of Rome or other earlier treaties and leglislations. These are initially for a common foreign policy and ultimately for the political union of the members of the EEC. These matters are dealt with under Title 111 of the SEA. Different constitutional procedures were required under the Irish Constitution for the ratification of the two parts of what is somewhat misleadingly called the Single European Act.

Titles I and II required amendment to existing legislation. This is done through the normal legislative process of introducing a Bill which, passing through the various stages in the Dail and Senate, is finally signed by the President and becomes law. The procedure for dealing with Title III, which is a matter of foreign policy, is laid down in Article 29 of the Constitution, which states (Section 5.1): "Every international agreement to which the State becomes a party shall be laid before Dail Eireann". The agreement is then approved or disapproved simply by a motion of the Dail.

Both parts of the SEA appeared to me to be unconstitutional. Titles I and II appeared to be unconstitutional in that this part of the SEA extended the scope of the EEC's capacity to intervene in Irish affairs beyond the limits set out by the Treaty of Accession of 1972 and by the amendment to the Constitution following the Referendum of that year. Title III appeared to be unconstitutional in that it involved a development of external relations which went well beyond the limits set down in the Constitution.

Other aspects of the SEA caused concern to others. The possibility that because of the SEA, EEC courts might legitimize abortion in Ireland aroused the opposition of those persons who feared for fundamental personal rights and who had succeeded in getting abortion made unconstitutional as well as illegal in the referendum of 1983. These were largely the same people who had defeated the constitutional amendment to permit divorce in 1986. I had voted against the amendment to make divorce constitutional on the grounds that to do so would destroy the power and right of young people to enter into legally binding, life-long contracts of marriage. If divorce were legalised, then marriage would be not "until death" but "until the divorce courts do us part". Persuaded after 40 years of marriage that a life-long union is much the best in most cases, it seemed important not to destroy, by legitimizing divorce, the right of young people to enter into legally binding contracts for such a union. Irrational as it may seem, the fact of entering into a legally binding contract of life-long marriage, plus all the other ballyhoo of weddings, appears to raise the probability that people would remain married for life. And that, if not always paradise, appears in most cases to be better than any available alternative. Legitimizing divorce would destroy the right of young people to enter into what on cold reflection seems a crazy contract of life-long marriage, but which magically appears to enhance the chances of achieving such a union.

There are other less damaging ways already available in Ireland of coping with broken marriages. One such way is for people, rationally concerned about the possibility of a breakup, to enter into a terminable contract of marriage in a solicitor's office, which, during its currency, confers the status of a regular marriage, including legitimacy on the offspring of the union. This option might be expanded into a more regular "second division", conditional form of wedding ceremony which would leave those who opted for it free to divorce while preserving the existing "first division", life-long union.

Relief of course is desirable for people whose marriage is broken irretrievably. It is important that legal separation, which defends the right of each party to escape the other, should be available to all who need it. The offspring of later, common law alliances, as indeed of all alliances out of wedlock, should be relieved of any surviving barbaric stigmas of illegitimacy. But as to the balance of convenience between the relatively few separated persons now "living in sin" and wishing to have their positions regularized, on the one hand, and the right of all young people stupidly, crazily, gloriously and in very many cases successfully, to enter into life-long contracts of marriage, I had no difficulty in making a decision.

Biddy, my wife, made a different decision and said she was voting for divorce! I failed to persuade her, as on many other matters during 40 years of nevertheless happy marriage, that as our votes would cancel out we should not bother to vote. She probably felt I would cheat by slipping in to vote against divorce while she refrained from voting for it!

While finding myself on the side of Family Solidarity, SPUC and such groups, I was not profoundly concerned with the possible threat to the fundamental rights of the unborn child which the SEA might carry. Those threats were hypothetical and abstract by comparison with what for long has been my principal preoccupation: the denial of a livelihood

91

to half the people born in Ireland, sustained through a century of colonial government and 65 years of native government. The element in those threats that did rankle was that, if the Irish in their wisdom or foolishness gave themselves certain laws, it was for the Irish alone to change those laws. It was intolerable that the laws of a former capitalist colony should be changed simply to bring them into line with those of the former imperial powers. That appeared to be a subversion of national democracy.

Again the threat to Irish neutrality and of nuclear conflagration inherent in the SEA caused me little trouble. By comparison with the real and actual denial of a livelihood to half the Irish people, these dangers and threats seemed remote, hypothetical and a luxury engaged in for the most part by persons removed from the reality of life without a job and without the self-respect that goes with a job. My objection was that under the EEC Ireland, the only former capitalist colony in Europe, would be aligning itself before the world in matters of foreign policy with the nine capitalist nations which between them colonised most of the non-European world and which left as their heritage the undeveloping Third World.

Ireland belongs to two worlds. Geographically it is part of Europe, the heritage of which it shares and to which in the past it contributed substantially. Historically it is part of the Third World, sharing with it over the past five centuries the common, traumatic experience of capitalist colonization. That dual character may well be a source of creative imagination and accounts perhaps for Ireland's extraordinarily rich literary output. It also gives Ireland a unique opportunity, and a correspondingly unique responsibility, to interpret the West to the Third World and the Third World to the West. It is this dual heritage that singles Ireland out as being the only former capitalist colony with a prospect of transforming economic undevelopment into development. If that precedent were once created, the other former capitalist colonies might then proceed to end economic undevelopment worldwide by their own efforts and not as a result of aid, advice or other forms of invariably harmful western intervention. Ireland in this way has now got the opportunity to repeat on a far vaster scale the greatest glories of its past.

There were in this context serious disadvantages in Ireland becoming, under the SEA, more closely identified with the Community of former capitalist colonial powers. First and foremost, that closer identity fostered the dependence which looked to EEC grants and to foreign credits to cope with our problems, in flagrant contradiction of the spirit of self-reliance, of sinn fein (by ourselves alone), which lay at the heart of Irish nationalism. To that extent the closer identification under the SEA of Ireland with the community of former capitalist colonial powers would vitiate or delay a resurgence of national self-respect and self-reliance. These qualities I perceived to be essential if Ireland, now that the state's credit was virtually exhausted and the casualties of a hopelessly flawed socio-economic order could no longer easily flow abroad, was not to collapse into the chaos common to the other former capitalist colonies which comprise the Third World.

The closer identification of Ireland with the Community of former capitalist colonial powers under the SEA would also lessen the beneficial, Third Worldwide impact Ireland might otherwise exert if perchance it transformed economic undevelopment into development. The more closely Ireland becomes identified in foreign affairs with the former capitalist colonial powers, the less clearly will it be perceived in the Third World as having an identity different from that of those powers, one that has much in common with the other former capitalist colonies of the Third World. Therefore, even if Ireland transformed economic undevelopment into development, the other undeveloping, former capitalist colonies of the Third World would see this as a purely Western phenomenon without relevance to the Third World. Ireland's historic opportunity of saving not only itself but, in doing so, of setting the essential precedent for the undeveloping half of the world to save itself from the chaos of undevelopment, would thus be jeopardised by the SEA.

These then were the harmful consequences which I perceived would flow from the ratification of the SEA:

    (i) a significant departure from constitutional government and the rule of law which could in time facilitate the imposition in Ireland of the illegitimate, dictatorial governments that are the norm in other former capitalist colonies;

(ii) further economic deterioration and accentuated dependence as the small peripheral Irish economy becomes more closely integrated into the core economy of the former capitalist colonial powers;

(iii) the possibility of having certain values which are widely held in the Community of former capitalist colonial powers superimposed on Ireland whether or not its people agreed with these;

(iv) jeopardizing Ireland's opportunity to play a key role in saving the Third World from the chaos of economic undevelopment, as it once saved continental Europe from the chaos of barbarism.

CHAPTER 5

Holding Back the Tide

A Reluctant Hero

The Irish political establishment, in the mid-1980s, was more discredited than it had ever been. In the autumn of 1986 the coalition government was on the point of collapse, its hair-shirt policies having failed not only to halt but even to slow the treadmill of a growing public debt with its attendant crippling service charges. The opposition Fianna Fail party had also exhausted its credibility and could offer no plausible alternative. The political Establishment was running out of steam. An attack on the SEA that was even partly successful might release more steam and therefore hasten change. It would cast doubt on the Irish government's ability to deliver even the minimal services of a client, which is a prompt response to the dictates of its patrons. If Irish governments could not be relied upon quickly and regularly to fall into line with the wishes of their EEC pay-masters, then perhaps there would be less incentive to continue the EEC doles on which the Irish economy had been made dependent. This desirable result might follow if Ireland did not duly ratify the SEA by 31 December 1986, causing the whole programme and schedule of the EEC to be disrupted. Preventing the ratification on schedule of the SEA treaty could also act as a rallying point for the many disparate elements within Ireland who, for one reason or another, were prepared to look beyond self to the greater good of society.

The Irish government had agreed to ratify the SEA before the end of 1986 so as to allow the Treaty to come into operation throughout the EEC on 1 January 1987. But the new EEC treaty raised clear constitutional issues. Given the jealous character of the Irish Constitution, which reflects Ireland's distinctive history of being Europe's only former capitalist colony, the only safe procedure by which Ireland could ratify the SEA was by first securing a constitutional amendment to allow the government to do so. Had that procedure been followed, the arrangements for holding a referendum could have easily been made in March 1986 and the referendum itself held in mid-summer. That would have permitted a full and orderly public debate on the issue, which would indubitably have included a comprehensive review of Ireland's membership of the EEC since 1972. It is unclear what Fianna Fail's attitude would have been in that case. In view of the party's opposition to the SEA when it was being debated, though not voted on, in Dail Eireann it seems probable that Fianna Fail would have acted in relation to a Coalition-sponsored referendum on the SEA as it had earlier on the divorce referendum: that is, it would not have opposed it but neither would it have supported it. It would have been, so to speak,"neutral against" the SEA. It is impossible to say what would have been the outcome of a referendum on the SEA conducted under such circumstances.

The coalition government led by Dr. Garret FitzGerald did not, however, proceed to hold a referendum along these lines. The Taoiseach's experience with referenda had been less than successful. An anti-abortion amendment was launched by an unwilling Garret FitzGerald in 1983 and he was a disappointed witness to its passage by a two to one majority on a turnout of 55% of the electorate. Again, his Government and the pro-divorce lobby had been defeated by a two to one majority on a turnout of 63% in the divorce amendment of 1986. Given these defeats and given the low morale of establishment politics, it was understandable if not commendable that the government should attempt to have the SEA ratified on a nod-and-a-wink so to speak, instead of through the due process of a referendum to amend the Constitution. By thus attempting to short-circuit what the Treaty of Rome refers to as "the due constitutional procedure" of the Irish state, the Government was giving hostages to fortune. It was leaving itself, the State and the EEC exposed to challenge in the Irish courts, which if successful would damage the government's reputation, lower Ireland's prestige and seriously inconvenience the European Community.

The possibility of at least preventing the ratification on schedule of the SEA emerged more clearly during the summer and autumn of 1986 as public debate on the subject developed. The principal credit for opening and pursuing that debate belongs to Anthony Coughlan.

I first met Anthony Coughlan in 1969, when Ireland had already agreed in principle to enter the EEC and a few of us were organising opposition to that entry. He and I had been active in the Common Market Defence Campaign to oppose entry to the EEC in 1972. After that I reverted to what I perceived to be the main task of studying and explaining Ireland's economic undevelopment, whereas Anthony, with Micheal O'Loinsigh and others, metamorphosed the CMDC into the Irish Sovereignty Movement.

Kind, considerate and courteous, Anthony Coughlan nevertheless has an iron will, formidable intellectual and organisational powers, and boundless energy to enforce that will. He has constantly and single-mindedly sought what he has perceived to be the wellbeing of the Irish nation. Partition, what is now frequently referred to as transnational capitalism, and membership of the EEC he has always regarded as incompatible with that wellbeing. Because of his conviction of the antipathy between EEC membership and the wellbeing of the country, he has from the beginning been by far the most implacable opponent of that membership. It was he more than anyone else who opened up the debate on the SEA and placed it centre-stage in Irish politics where it could not possibly get through on a nod-and-a-wink.

The Labour Party, Garret FitzGerald's partner in office, had meanwhile got itself into difficulties over the SEA. The four Labour ministers had approved it in cabinet despite the opposition of rank-and-file members and the party's affiliated trade unions. Labour's annual conference was due to be held in early November and there were resolutions on the agenda calling on the Labour TDs not to vote to ratify the SEA. In view of party feeling, there was every likelihood of these being adopted, which would have made it impossible for the

Coalition to continue. There was deep concern among the Labour Party leaders at the prospect of loss of office. Then the accident of a strike of cleaning staff at Cork City Hall, where the conference was to be held, provided the ministers with the weak excuse they needed to call off the conference. No other hall in the country, apparently, would suit as an alternative venue! Then, having promised the party's Administrative Council that no decision would be taken until the party members had a say on the matter, the Labour TDs trooped with Fine Gael through the Dail lobbies to ratify the SEA. Labour's 1986 annual conference was never held. The coalition held together and office was enjoyed for another three months. Even by the standards of Ireland's corrupt party politics, this was an exceptionally cynical abuse of power that will have contributed further to undermining public respect for the political establishment.

The following letter, which Anthony Coughlan was instrumental in drafting, was published in the Irish national daily newspapers on 10 November 1986 and gave substance to the view that Dr. FitzGerald's Government were acting illegally:

Sir,

As lawyers, we wish to express our public concern as to whether the correct constitutional procedure is being followed in relation to the ratification by the Oireachtas of the Single European Act, the treaty which the Government signed with our fellow EEC members earlier this year. This is quite apart from any views we may have as individuals concerning the intrinsic merits or demerits of this measure.

Article 29.4.3 of the Constitution, on the basis of which Ireland was enabled to join the EEC following the referendum of 1972, reads, inter alia: "No provision of this Constitution invalidates laws enacted, acts done or measures adopted by the State necessitated by the obligations of membership of the Communities, or prevents laws enacted, acts done or measures adopted by the Communities, or institutions thereof from having the force of law in the State".

It is on the basis of this constitutional amendment

that Community legislation is enabled to be part of the domestic law of the State. The European Communities (Amendment) Bill 1986, whose proposed adoption by the Oireachtas would make the relevant provisions of the Single European Act part of our domestic law, gives novel and additional legislative and executive competence to the Community institutions, the Council of Ministers and the Commission, over and above that possessed by the European Communities we agreed to join in 1972. It does so by adding new treaty articles dealing with new subject matter, for example technology and environment, to the Treaty of Rome and by altering several existing articles to allow for the relevant Community law to be made on a new basis, that is, by qualified majority vote rather than unanimously.

It is our view that these legislative changes are not legally "necessitated by the obligations of membership of the Communities" and are therefore not covered by the exemption provided in Article 29.4.3 of the Constitution. It would appear therefore that future Community law deriving from the changes in the Rome Treaty proposed in the Single European Act would be invalid unless a further constitutional amendment approved by the people were to permit this. Consequently the Oireachtas would be acting invalidly by passing the European Community (Amendment) Bill 1986 without a constitutional amendment being adopted first which gave it the proper authority. A bill should therefore be introduced for the holding of a referendum.

We emphasise again that we bring this matter to the attention of our legislators and the general public out of concern for the integrity of the Constitution, for the rights of the Irish people and for the competence of the Houses of the Oireachtas, quite apart from any view we may have on the content of the treaty for which the Government seeks approval.

Yours etc.

Kader Asmal (TCD)   Dr. Sean MacBride,SC
Rory Brady, BL, J. Paul McCutcheon (NIHE, Limerick)

Tom Cooney (UCD)   Gerard Meehan (NIHE, Limerick)
Professor Henry Ellis   Dr. Aindrias O Caoimh, BL
G.M. Golding (UCD)   Professor Paul O'Higgins (TCD)
Donnchadh D. Lehane   Seamas O Tuathail, BL
Professor Mary McAleese(TCD) Michael White (Solicitor)
Ferdinand Von Prondzynski (TCD).

The Irish Council of the European Movement, a purportedly independent organisation which is financed principally by the EEC, the Irish government and by foreign companies operating in Ireland, orchestrated the campaign to sell the SEA to the Irish public, and in the process to denigrate the opposition. A senior permanent official in the EEC section of the Department of Foreign Affairs, Mr. Michael Hoey, on leave of absence, attached himself to the ICEM to direct the marketing of the SEA. This, Mr. Sean MacBride S.C. pointed out, in his view breached the long-standing Irish (and British) convention that civil servants remain aloof from the hurly-burly of politics. But a government prepared to chance having the SEA ratified unconstitutionally and prepared to risk the ignominy of being stymied in that attempt, did not baulk at a civil servant on leave of absence heading their political campaign to sell the SEA to the Irish public.

Apart from granting Mr. Hoey leave of absence to head the ICEM, the government, after agreeing in February 1986 with the governments of the other states of the EEC to ratify the SEA before the end of the year, omitted to take any action until November. Then, in response to the growing public concern about the SEA, which had been initiated by the Irish Sovereignty Movement and by the Irish CND and had subsequently been taken up by the Fianna Fail party in opposition, the government published the "Blue Book", *The Single European Act: An Explanatory Guide*. This was a soporific interpretation of the SEA which suggested that there was nothing involved in it that had not already been provided for in the Treaty of Rome and the Treaty of Irish Accession to the EEC. It did, however, help to foster a greater public awareness and for the first time made easily available copies of the SEA.

It was clear by November that there was a groundswell of

opposition to the SEA. I would be by no means isolated in opposing a measure which, with increasing clarity, appeared to epitomise the failure of successive Irish governments to escape the heritage of capitalist colonialism and to transform undevelopment into development. This new EEC treaty was a substantial and unconstitutional step further down the road to dependence on grants and credits from outsiders and towards the further erosion of Irish sovereignty.

Paul Callan, S.C., was a critical element in that groundswell of opposition. Paul, who practised in the Northern Circuit, had come into public prominence for his involvement in two major cases, *Northern Bank v Charlton* and *Monaghan Hospital v Minister for Health*. He had been joined in the successful defence of Charlton by Mr. Don Barrington S.C., who was later elevated to the High Court and who figures prominently in this story. In the latter case, Paul Callan acted on behalf of 20,000 Monaghan people who objected to the Minister for Health closing their County Hospital. He succeeded in having the order closing the hospital struck down as *ultra vires* the relevant legislation. Both cases went to the Supreme Court; and in both cases Paul was opposed by T.K. Liston, S.C., the octogenarian doyen of the Irish Bar, who was also to confront him in the SEA litigation.

There were, of course, important political connotations in the Monaghan Hospital case. But Paul Callan, S.C. had evinced political involvement apart from this. He had stood unsuccessfully in the Louth constituency on behalf of the Labour Party in the General Election of 1969. Subsequently he had been many years on the Administrative Council of the Party. On a later occasion he had acted as election agent for a Fine Gael friend in a Monaghan by-election.

Paul Callan spoke to barrister Seamas O'Tuathail about the letter to the newspapers concerning the SEA which Seamas and a dozen other lawyers had signed. Paul concurred with the views expressed in the letter and wondered if anything was being done to challenge the ratification of the SEA. Seamas O'Tuathail in turn was aware of the interest of Mr. T.C.G. O'Mahoney in the question.

Mr. O'Mahoney, a prominent Dublin solicitor noted for his commitment to what many would regard as ultramontane

Catholic causes, had been concerned about the constitutionality of the SEA for some time and had interested another young lawyer, Miss Antonia O'Callaghan, B.L. Mr. Brendan O'Connor was another person who was concerned about legal and constitutional aspects of the SEA and he played an important part in lobbying various TDs when the matter came before the Dail.

In Cork, Joe Noonan and Mary Lenihan, a husband and wife team of solicitors who had been prominently associated with the Campaign for Nuclear Disarmament and its journal *Disarm*, were actively mobilising opinion. They were especially concerned about the foreign affairs and neutrality implications of the SEA.

Anthony Coughlan, as well as maintaining a barrage of letters to, and articles in, the press and addressing meeting after meeting on the SEA, was in contact with all of these disparate elements which were expressing opposition to the SEA. I in turn frequently met Anthony in Trinity College, where we both work.

The government, undeterred by the mounting opposition, prepared to proceed with legislation on the SEA in Dail Eireann on 9th December. Anthony Coughlan and I discussed the possibility of pre-empting the legislation to ratify the SEA by seeking a Court Order directing the government instead to hold a referendum. With the legislative process due to commence in the Dail on 9th December, the last day on which legal action to prevent its initiation was possible was 1 December. Yet though the matter had been frequently discussed, the serious decision to ask the High Court to direct the Government to proceed to a referendum on the SEA had not been taken by the end of November. Finally, on the last day of the month, Tony Coughlan phoned me at home to discuss the matter with a view to my initiating litigation that day. He told me that Mr. O'Mahoney was willing to make his services as a solicitor available.

Earlier in the day I had wrenched a muscle in my back, and in a manner which I have never before or since experienced was almost paralyzed by an acute bout of lumbago. The slightest movement in a warm bed was agony and even if the fate of Ireland depended upon my shifting from it - which the fate of Ireland did not - there was nothing I could do. For that day, but fortunately for that day alone, I was *hors de combat*.

There were several other phone calls from my bedside. The upshot of these was that late on the next evening, Tony Coughlan, T.C.G. O'Mahoney and a notary public attended my bedside, not to make my will, but to receive and to witness my formal instructions to initiate proceedings in the High Court with a view to obtaining an order directing the government to refrain from legislation to ratify the SEA without first holding a referendum. It was a false start. Mr O'Mahoney's request got short shrift from Justice Carroll. Further action along that course was clearly pointless.

It was now December and the SEA was due to come into operation throughout the EEC on 1 January following. To comply with its undertakings to the other governments of the EEC, the Irish government had to complete all the processes necessary for ratification during this final month of 1986. There were three barriers to implementation still to be surmounted. The first was getting the necessary legislation through the Oireachtas. The second was the possible reference of the legislation by the President to the Supreme Court to test its constitutionality. A third possible barrier was a challenge in the courts, by one or more citizens, to the legislation's constitutionality. In view of the importance and complexity of the legislation, of the country's commitment to the other member governments of the EEC, of the serious doubts that had been raised at an early stage about the constitutionality of the SEA, and of the need for a calm unhurried debate if there was to be a referendum, Garret FitzGerald's coalition government had been extremely remiss in not initiating the legislative process months earlier.

There appeared to be two explanations for this extraordinary dilatoriness. First, the Coalition was clearly coming apart. Its troubles were legion. In their concern to hold on to office, the government were prepared to put off for as long as possible - in this case until December 1986 - legislation of a contentious nature. Second, as mentioned already, Dr. FitzGerald's experiences with referenda had been unsatisfactory to say the least. These unpleasant experiences presumably made FitzGerald wary of referenda. It was understandable, if not commendable, that he should attempt to have the SEA ratified by the Dail at the last moment, in the dead of winter, perhaps hoping in this way to avoid another referendum and the possibility of a third referendum defeat.

But whatever about Dr. FitzGerald's views, I was by now committed to taking whatever action was open to a citizen to prevent or to delay the ratification of the SEA. The first thing to be done was to attempt to stiffen Oireachtas opposition to the measure. Accordingly I wrote to every member of the Dail and Senate as follows:

> 3,Willowfield Park, Dublin 14,
> 8th December, 1986.

Dear Deputy/Senator,

I am writing to you as a private citizen who is very concerned at the manner in which the Government are seeking to ratify the Single European Act and make it part of the domestic law of the State without reference to the people, which I believe is the only constitutional way this can be done.

As an economist and economic historian I have for many years been studying how Ireland and its citizens have been affected by the European Community. I believe that the Single European Act, which is an amendment to the Rome Treaty establishing the EEC, is a document transferring sovereignty and affecting citizens' rights. It is called a treaty, but is contrary to the Constitution. It extends the powers and functions of the EEC into new areas. I believe that this, together with the adoption of a new regime of general majority voting – in which Ireland will have three votes out of 76 – marks the effective end of Ireland's veto over large areas of EEC policy-making. It will have the most baneful effects over the coming decade on most people in this country. I believe that this treaty will adversely affect our sovereignty, our democracy, the character of our representative government, the constitutional rights of citizens, and the economic and social interests of most members of our community.

I have discussed this matter with people who are expert in economic, political and constitutional issues and they have confirmed my fears. I believe that many people share my view that the Constitution does not permit this treaty to be ratified in the way the Government proposes, because it diminishes our fundamental constitutional rights. The Single European Act goes far beyond what the Irish people consented to when they approved membership of the EEC in 1972. It purports to give powers, rights and law-making capacity to the EEC institutions, and to the State acting on their behalf, which go beyond those constitutionally or legally necessitated by the obligations of membership of the Communities we joined in 1973.

If implemented, I believe that the Single European Act and the laws which the EEC would consequently be empowered to make, will impinge on and destroy some of the fundamental personal and human rights guaranteed under the Constitution, not least the right to life which was confirmed in the constitutional amendment adopted by the people some time ago. I believe the Title III of the Single Act, which commits us to develop a common security and defence policy with the NATO members of the EEC, entails the surrender of a degree of independence and sovereignty which the Irish people have not assented to and which may only occur if they give assent by referendum. Moreover, the commitment we give in this treaty to work to maintain the technological and industrial basis of the security of the EEC states would, in my opinion, make it legally improper for Ireland to criticise such installations as Sellafield or other nuclear facilities which have objectively harmful effects on the population of this country, but which are regarded by our EEC partners as necessary for their security.

I appeal to you therefore and to your colleagues in the Oireachtas, to safeguard my constitutional rights and those of other citizens by insisting that the government introduce a Referendum Bill to confer the necessary powers on the Houses of the Oireachtas before calling on public representatives to ratify the Single European Act treaty in either its domestic or foreign policy parts. I appeal to you to reject the government's attempt to induce Deputies and Senators to give approval both to the treaty and to the European Communities Amendment Bill 1986 without consulting and getting the permission first of the people of Ireland.

Yours sincerely,
Raymond Crotty.

I followed up that letter with telephone calls to as many Opposition TDs as I could contact urging them to oppose the SEA. I submitted to Fianna Fail headquarters a memorandum on the implications of the SEA for changing the manner of decision-making on "measures concerned with the protection of savings, in particular the granting of credit and the exercise of the banking profession" from unanimity, as hitherto, to a qualified majority on the EECs Council of Ministers, in which Ireland has a mere three votes out of a total of 76.

Simultaneously, I instructed Mr. O'Mahoney to consult Paul Callan S.C. on the possibility of litigation to challenge the constitutionality of the SEA, should the Oireachtas pass the legislation and should the President not refer it to the Supreme Court. A number of lengthy consultations followed at which erudite submissions on various aspects of the complex Treaty were considered. Particularly useful in this respect was a submission by Brendan O'Connor on the implications of the SEA for the fundamental rights enshrined in the Constitution; and a submission by Mary Lenihan and Joe Noonan on Title III, dealing with foreign policy and neutrality.

Grattan Healy, a member of the Green Alliance, had by now helped to form a broad coalition of left of centre groupings called CREST – the Campaign for the Renegotiation of the SEA. This included people from the Labour Left, the Workers' Party, the Irish Sovereignty Movement and a number of trade unions. It had begun actively to campaign against the SEA, holding meetings and canvassing.

Simultaneously work was in progress to mobilize persons more closely identified with the centre of Irish politics. This became the Constitutional Rights Campaign, under the joint chairmanship of Professor Mary McAleese and Mr. John Carroll. Mary McAleese is a Professor of Law at Trinity College Dublin and had been associated with Family Solidarity in the divorce referendum. John Carroll, of course, is the President of the Irish Transport and General Workers Union, the largest trade union in Ireland. He was also President of the Irish Congress of Trade Unions, which had opposed ratification of the SEA at its annual conference in Belfast the previous summer.

CREST and CRC, as well as mobilizing public opinion, had

also commenced on the critically important work of getting funds to finance resistance to the SEA. These funds were needed immediately to cover the cost of holding public meetings, having posters and leaflets printed and, in the case of the CRC, renting an office in St. Andrews Street, Dublin 2. Less immediately there was the possibility of a referendum, and funds would be needed to make a fight of that. Meanwhile, however, I had been assured that, for what they were worth, any funds collected by the Constitutional Rights Campaign would be available as a contribution to my legal costs should I decide to challenge the SEA in the courts.

Any financial help from CRC obviously would be most welcome. Though unlikely to amount to more than a small fraction of the total costs of litigation taken unsuccessfully all the way to the Supreme Court, it would, and did, cover the out-of-pocket expenses of even considering a major court case. It was important, therefore, to secure and retain the support of CRC, CREST and any other organizations willing to help, but this support was threatened by Mr. O'Mahoney's involvement in the case. A most able, trenchant opponent of the SEA, who had been largely instrumental in creating an awareness of the possibility of challenging it in the courts, Mr. O'Mahoney had strong religious views which he did not hesitate to express. While not necessarily dissenting from Mr. O'Mahoney's views, nor of course questioning his right to express them, it seemed to me as the case developed that it would be prudent, given its highly political nature, to change to a solicitor of less pronounced views, less forcefully expressed. Reluctantly I decided to transfer the case from Mr. O'Mahoney's offices, where we had been most competently and courteously treated.

My attempt to persuade Dail Eireann to reject the SEA was as effective as an airgun pellet on an elephant's hide. Though trenchant criticism of the SEA was expressed, particularly by Mr. Haughey and by some others in the Party, at the crucial Second Reading in the Dail, Fianna Fail refrained from challenging a division on the Treaty. Ostensibly this was because, as Fianna Fail subsequently put it, "in the situation this government have created there is (no) alternative to ratifying".

But as everyone knew and as the Chief Whip of the Fianna Fail party, Mr. Brady, had said to me, the real reason was because of the possibility of defeating the SEA, which would have precipitated a General Election. A General Election on the SEA or on the issue of being in or out of the EEC would have provided the coalition government with the best chance it would ever have of being re-elected.

With the passage of the SEA through the Oireachtas, only two barriers remained to its ratification. The first of these was a Presidential referral to the Supreme Court and the second was a constitutional challenge by a citizen in the courts. If necessary I was prepared to make that challenge, though if others wished to do so I would have been perfectly happy to leave it to them. The important thing was to make the challenge competently; which citizen or group of citizens did so was unimportant. But given the considerable likelihood of losing the case, it would have been pointless for more than one citizen to make the challenge, for in the event of defeat the costs to be met would be enormous, far more than I could pay. There was simply no point in more than one person being bankrupted.

Objectively, there was a case for me rather than another challenging the SEA in the Courts. One qualification was my lack of political connections. I did try to follow my brother Martin into the Blueshirts, as into most things, in the 1930s. There must have been a lower age limit of ten years, for while Martin was accepted as a member and got a very snazzy looking blue shirt, with epaulettes, pockets and other trimmings, I, who was two years younger, was not accepted. By good fortune rather than good judgment, I never after joined, or attempted to join, any of the political parties which between them have brought the country to the brink of catastrophe. I could not, therefore, be accused of grinding a party political, or other, axe. I could sincerely and honestly claim to be Sean Citizen, concerned as much as, but no more than, his fellows about the consequences for me and other citizens of the ratification of the SEA.

The President cannot, according to the Constitution, sign a Bill into law earlier than five days after it has passed through the Dail and Senate. He must sign a Bill within seven days of its passing through the Oireachtas, unless he refers it to the Supreme Court for a judgment on its constitutionality. As soon as the President signed the European Communities (Amendment) Bill 1986 enacting the SEA into law, the instrument of ratification could be lodged with the Government of Italy, which acted as custodian of documents pertaining to the EEC's founding Treaty of Rome and amending Treaties. Once the instrument of ratification of the SEA was so lodged, the constitutional position would be transformed, for then the SEA would be covered by the same immunity to constitutional challenge as was enjoyed by the 1972 Treaty of Accession and measures enacted under it. This immunity was conferred by the 1972 amendment to the Constitution which added Article 29.4.3: "The State may become a member of the European Coal and Steel Community (established by Treaty signed at Paris on 18th April, 1951), the European Economic Community (established by Treaty signed at Rome on 25th day of March, 1957) and the European Atomic Energy Committee (established by Treaty signed at Rome on 25th day of March, 1957). No provision of this Constitution invalidates laws enacted, acts done or measures adopted by the State necessitated by the obligations of membership of the Communities or prevents laws enacted, acts done or measures adopted by the Communities, or its institutions thereof, from having the force of law in the State."

These constitutional procedures created a problem. On the one hand, the legislative process could not be said to be completed for five days after the Act had been passed to the President for signing into law. In accordance with the fundamental constitutional doctrine of the division of legislative, executive and judicial powers, we would have got short shrift from any judge we might approach for an injunction to halt the legislative process. Effectively that would have meant injuncting the President in the course of legislation, a constitutionally unheard of thing. On the other hand, if we delayed for more than seven days, the President would have been bound to sign the European Communities (Amendment) Bill 1986 (comprising Title II of the SEA) into law. He would also, on the advice of the government, have signed the instrument of ratification of the SEA, which would then have been lodged with the Italian government. Once that occurred, there would have been no possibility of redress for us.

There is no formal channel through which citizens can learn when a particular piece of legislation is passed to the President for his consideration and signature. We did, however, learn informally that the European Communities (Amendment) Bill 1986 had been placed before the President on 18 December, which meant that he could not sign it into law before 23rd December; and he had to do so before 25th December if he chose not to refer it for a decision to the Supreme Court. The instrument of ratification of the SEA had to be signed by the President before 31st December to comply with the government's undertaking to the governments of the other EEC member states. Our time for action was thus narrowed down to the 23rd December.

Paul Callan, S.C., assisted by Antonia O'Callaghan and Seamas O'Tuathail as junior counsel, and instructed by Messrs Moylan Whitaker, solicitors on my behalf, prepared to seek an injunction preventing the state and the government from lodging the instrument of ratification with the government of Italy. As I understood the situation, it was without precedent to injunct government in the prosecution of public business or the state itself in relation to an international treaty. I may injunct my neighbour if he is, for example, making alterations to his house which seemed to endanger my property. A court may grant me an order prohibiting him from proceeding with the alterations until the issue has been tried in court to establish whether there is substance in my claim.

The approach in relation to government is different. There is here a constitutional presumption that government is acting legally and therefore is not trespassing on the citizen's rights. Only if that assumption is invalidated by the facts subsequently can the citizen seek redress against the government. It can always be safely assumed that because of the government's limitless resources it, unlike the ordinary citizen, will be able to compensate for whatever damage may have been done the injured citizen. But a key point in our case was that once the ratification of the SEA was completed, by the lodgment of the instrument with the Italian government, I could no longer look for redress from the Irish courts. Any redress I might henceforth seek in relation to the SEA would have to be from the European Court of Justice. That body is not subject to the Irish Constitution. In this instance, therefore, if my rights as a citizen under the Constitution were to be protected, government unprecedentedly would have to be injuncted in the course of pursuing its international business.

Matters were not simplified by the close approach of Christmas, which meant that the courts had adjourned for the holidays. On Monday 22nd December, when the lawyers prepared to seek a High Court injunction, they discovered that Mr. Justice McKenzie, who had been designated Duty Judge to deal with emergencies during the holidays, was unavailable through illness. They therefore enquired about the availability of Miss Justice Carroll, who, because of her involvement with Mr. O'Mahoney's application early in December, had some knowledge of the matter. But she also was unavailable. The choice then fell on Justice Barrington, a person reputed especially knowledgeable in constitutional law. Justice Barrington agreed to hear the application. These details are important in view of the allegation made subsequently by the State that we had engaged in "forum shopping", or looking around for a "soft touch" judge.

As well as ensuring that a High Court judge would be available when the time for action came the lawyers, Paul Callan, Antonia O'Callaghan and Seamas O'Tuathail (barristers) and Declan Moylan (solicitor), during Monday 22nd December, prepared the case for seeking the injunction.

On Monday evening at 7 p.m., the legal team drove from Moylan Whitaker's office in Baggot Street to Justice Barrington's residence. They were accompanied by a relief car in case, at that more than usually dangerous hour in an accident-prone season, any mishap occurred to the first car. At midnight on 22nd December it could be said that the legislative process of ratifying the SEA was completed. The President would now be free to sign the Bill into law and also sign the instrument of ratification which government could then lodge with the government of Italy. My rights under the Irish Constitution therefore depended on the intervention of the Irish courts. Justice Barrington, summoned from his family

111

fireplace in the late evening of 22nd December, received the lawyers courteously. He heard their two-hour outline of the situation on affidavit and agreed to hear our case for an injunction at a special vacation sitting of the High Court to be convened at the Four Courts at 12 noon on the following day.

The Chief State Solicitor had now to be notified so that the government side could appear in court to answer our claim for an injunction. It was our responsibility to find and inform him. The police in Cabinteely tried his home, but he was out. Various parties and governmental jollifications around town were checked out. Eventually he was tracked down around midnight and told of Justice Barrington's decision to hold a hearing twelve hours later. A letter was also dropped into the Attorney General's house in Rathgar. Over the next few hours of darkness officials and lawyers were summoned from pre-Christmas bibulations throughout Dublin's south side to assemble at the Foreign Affairs Department in Iveagh House, Stephen's Green. Motorcars rolled up outside and the windows lighted up as the government side laboured into the morning preparing a reply to this seemingly quite unexpected legal pitfall, for the timing of which the government was itself entirely responsible.

I joined the lawyers and their advisors who had assembled at Moylan Whitaker's office at 9 a.m. on Tuesday 23rd December. There was much hurried last-minute consultation and preparation of additional affidavits, all of which I watched agape with the wonder proper to any layperson when experts are engaged in complex matters of great importance. Finally the party, laden with files, legal texts and tomes of court reports to be quoted for precedent if necessary, took off in several cars for the Four Courts.

Like every Irish person, I knew the Four Courts on Dublin's Liffeyside. Its architecture was sufficiently striking – the pillared portico and the oxygenized, green copper dome. That architecture had been restored since the burning of the Four Courts, which was the opening encounter of the sordid civil war of 1922-23. I was especially aware that in the burning of the Four Courts a large proportion of Ireland's ancient public records had been destroyed. This was a loss for which I grieved because of the paramount importance of the historical approach to understanding economics. But like most Irish people that was about all I knew of the place. I had never passed through its impressive portico before 23rd December 1986. During the coming months I was to become very familiar with it indeed.

In retrospect I recognize that there had been quite an achievement between midnight and 12 noon. The legal process, which like much of the nation was in mid-winter dormancy, had been suddenly awakened from hibernation; and here promptly at 12 noon it was ready for action. It was, however, very much a holiday job, as I was to learn subsequently. The foyer, under the imposing copper dome, was empty but for a couple of attendants, whereas when the Courts are in regular session it is athrong with people at that hour, just before the hearings commence. The action was concentrated that morning in High Court No. 4. Within it a somewhat motley group assembled, which included the lawyers on both sides, a couple of press reporters, I the plaintiff, and at the stroke of twelve Judge Barrington. All were wigless and in mufti to assert that we were still on our Christmas holidays, but taking time off to deal with a troublesome matter that required immediate attention. For one thing in particular I was grateful: the court, on that dark, cold, wet mid-winter day, was comfortably heated. That seemed no small achievement, given that the whole matter had been set in train only twelve hours earlier. It continued likewise to be pleasantly heated throughout the proceedings, prompting my daughter Anne on one occasion, when she accompanied her Mum and myself to the Court, to hope for Mum's sake that the case would last until the warm weather came!

In these days of television series like *Matlock* and *Rumpole of the Bailey*, everyone is aware of court procedure. It was not difficult to follow the case, but I nevertheless failed to pick up several important nuances which Junior Counsel Antonia O'Callaghan or Seamas O'Tuathail kindly explained to me subsequently.

I was not, however, quite such "a dull and muddly-mettled fellow" as to be impervious to the attacks launched on our case on 24th December by Mr. Eoghan FitzSimons, S.C., counsel for the defendant, who in this case was the State, the

Government and the Attorney General. That was especially because a good deal of Mr. FitzSimons's attacks were directed against me. The attacks, if on reflection no sharper than the occasion warranted, did hurt at the time and suggested that I was a crank, a person of no standing, or in legal jargon lacking *locus standi;* and that I had no business being in court asking a judge to injunct the duly elected government of the land. Much of the state's case centred on the assertion that the Irish Government had given a formal undertaking to the other eleven governments of the EEC that the SEA would be ratified before the end of December so that its provisions could come into operation as scheduled on 1 January, 1987. Mr. FitzSimons emphasized that 320 million Europeans, twelve governments and the EEC Commission were "raring to go" on the SEA and that it would be quite improper for Judge Barrington to thwart them at the behest of a crank without *locus standi.* To do so could have the gravest consequences for Ireland, which depended so very greatly on the goodwill of its EEC partners. Mr. Callan, in reply, observed that the 320 million Europeans might find much to admire in the working of the Irish Courts and Constitution!

Mr. FitzSimons, in the course of arguing the state's defence on the second day of hearing, Christmas Eve, mentioned that the President had that morning signed the Bill that brought Titles I and II of the SEA into law. Later in the day he informed the Court that the President, acting on the advice of the Government, had signed the Dail motion relating to Title III of the SEA. Everything was now in order to ratify it in accordance with the government's undertaking of the previous February to our EEC partners.

This latter intervention was, in my view, highly improper. Judgment on my application for an injunction would be delivered that day. That would still leave a week in which the President could have signed the instrument and had it lodged with the Italian government by 31st December in accordance with Ireland's commitments. The government, by advising the President to sign the instrument on 24th December and informing the court that he had done so, was in effect putting a gun to Justice Barrington's head. They were now placing the whole onus of delaying ratification of a treaty involving twelve governments and 320 million people on one man. The executive was failing lamentably to display "that respect which one great organ of state owes to another", of which much was to be heard in the Four Courts during the coming weeks.

To drive home the enormity of the imbalance between the interests of twelve governments, the EEC Commission and 320 million people and the plaintiff, Mr. FitzSimons at this juncture brought out the point that not only was I a crank without *locus standi,* but I had moreover engaged in the sneaky business of "forum shopping". For had I not shopped around for a judge who would be a soft touch?

The case was adjourned at what, in my view, is the very worst hour of the year: 5 p.m. on 24 December – invariably cold, wet and dismal outside; and not late enough to sit in beside a glowing fire. Justice Barrington said he would prepare his judgment and deliver it in an hour's time when the Court would reassemble.

A stroll up to Bewleys in Westmoreland Street seemed a good idea to get away from the tension in Court No. 4; a cup of coffee and an eclair would be welcome nourishment. At the pedestrian crossing outside the Olympia Theatre in Dame Street, Mr. FitzSimons was waiting for a break in the traffic at what is possibly the most accident-prone hour in the year. I joined him and in the spirit of the season advised him not to take a chance with the traffic. I added that it was even more important that I should do likewise since, I understood, that if the approaching juggernaut squashed the life out of me that would be the end of the case now before the court. And so much hard work by the lawyers would be wasted!

Later that evening, walking up Kildare Street to catch a homeward-bound 62 bus on St. Stephen's Green, I perceived a figure emerging from Leinster House who might have been Peter Barry, Minister for Foreign Affairs, the man responsible for getting the SEA ratified. The Peter-Barry-like figure was accosted by a couple of acquaintances outside Leinster House who engaged him in conversation. On approaching it became clear that it was indeed, without his state car, Peter Barry, whom I had never before seen in person and who had certainly never seen me apart from photographs in that day's newspapers. Quite spontaneously we grinned at each other and wished one another a happy Christmas!

I have already referred to the impressive manner in which the logistics of a High Court sitting had been speedily and effectively set in train following the visit to the Judge's residence two evenings earlier. But now a gap appeared in the provisions which had been so swiftly and efficiently arranged. There was no stenographer to capture for posterity what was to be a historic judgment and which indeed Judge Barrington suggested should be recorded. Without a stenographer the judgment would become part of the folklore but not the record of the Irish legal system. But the resources of the state could not rise to a stenographer at 5 p.m. on Christmas Eve. Messengers on the plaintiff's side scurried in various directions seeking a stenographer; and failing a stenographer, a tape-recorder. Seamas O'Tuathail, more mobile than the rest of us on his faithful bicycle, brought back the loot: the last tape-recorder for sale in Capel Street as stocks vanished in the last hour of the last day of shopping before Christmas. The apparatus was rigged up in Court No. 4 and Judge Barrington good-humouredly interrupted his delivery periodically to allow tapes to be replaced.

The judgment, which was the first I had ever heard delivered, amazed me. There had been two full days of hearings. Innumerable points had been made. Complex arguments pro and contra had been submitted by counsel who were masters of their work. What would have been for me and for most lay people a jumbled mass had been sorted out, each submission, argument and counter-argument considered and filed away by a brilliant legal mind into its appropriate place in a thematic jigsaw. This was a jigsaw such as Judge Barrington himself referred to in his judgment when describing the process of ratification of the SEA: "In other words, once all the pieces of the jigsaw puzzle are in place it would appear to follow that the obligation to observe the provisions of the European Act would be one of the obligations of the European Court and would have validity within the jurisdiction of this country in the domestic law of this country by virtue of the provisions of the Third Amendment to the Constitution".

I had been studying the SEA carefully for almost a year. It

had been my principal preoccupation since early November and my sole preoccupation for a month. At the end of two days' argument in the High Court, all was confusion. I needed time to sort matters out. But here was a Judge, who two days earlier presumably knew no more about the SEA than any layperson, after a day and a half's hearing and an hour's contemplation giving a clear, reasoned exposition of the legal and constitutional implications of the SEA's ratification. It was one of the most impressive intellectual performances I have witnessed. It induced in me a new and higher regard for the legal profession; and especially for those at the apex of it in this country's judiciary. I would like to think that this opinion has not been influenced by the nature of Justice Barrington's judgment.

Justice Barrington found that, on balance, the danger of my constitutional rights being irretrievably lost by the ratification of the SEA outweighed the embarrassment to government of failing to ratify the treaty before 31st December as agreed; and outweighed also any annoyance caused to those 320 million Europeans who, according to counsel for the defence, were all so eager to ratify and implement the SEA. At the end of the forty-minute judgment, I heard the magic words from Judge Barrington: "I accordingly will grant the interlocutory injunction sought by the plaintiff".

My legal acquaintances assure me that Judge Barrington's judgment will go into the record as a classic among Irish court judgments. It broke important new ground in Irish constitutional law. For the first time an Irish court had halted the state and the process of government in its tracks. Prior to this the courts had scrupulously refrained from even considering what the executive arm of government was about. Only when legislation was in place and an aggrieved citizen complained that it impinged on his or her constitutional rights would the courts intervene. Then, if they thought the situation merited it, they would strike down the legislation as being unconstitutional. Government, in that event, would have the choice of abandoning the legislation or of seeking to amend the Constitution by referendum. The court had created a major precedent on this occasion by striking down an international treaty before it was fully in place – while, so to speak, it was in mid-air between Aras an Uachtarain and the Quirinal Palace in Rome.

Great was the jubilation in the camp. In the funereal gloom of the foyer of the locked Four Courts on Christmas Eve, a few of us jigged a few steps and others looked as if they might easily do so but for the weight of their vast legal erudition. Magically the dark wet coldness of the mid-winter Dublin evening had given way to a warm, brilliant inner sunshine. Anthony Coughlan, who was at the Four Courts from the beginning of the proceedings and who was not to miss a day of the main action, was delighted. The judgment was, he declared, the best Christmas present he had ever received. That, I learnt subsequently, was precisely how a famous politician, waiting impatiently in Kinsealy to gather into his hands the reins of Irish political power, also saw the injunction when he was told about it that evening.

For my part the effort and the risk had been fully justified regardless of further proceedings. The Irish government could not now fulfil its undertaking to the other EEC member governments to ratify the SEA before the end of 1986. All the other member states had ratified the SEA; Ireland was odd man out, as I wished it to be. Even if we paused for a mere month at this milestone on the road to further dependence on, and integration with, the EEC, much was gained.

CHAPTER 6

Their Hands in the Till

There was, however, little time for resting on laurels or even celebrating Christmas. Judge Barrington allowed the barest minimum time to prepare the substantive case. We were given seven days to prepare a Statement of Claim and the state a further seven days to prepare its Reply. Like Cinderella we had to get, by midnight on New Year's Eve 1986, our detailed case against the Single European Act into the hands of the state's Solicitor General.

I did not go chasing the wren that Stephen's Day; nor do much else for the remainder of that year but remain closeted with the lawyers working on the case. That was in Paul Callan's flat in Merrion Court. Over Christmas there was a break-in at Moylan Whitaker's offices in Baggot Street. With memories of Watergate still fresh and with a healthy respect for the initiative of our own Special Branch, the risk that the offices might have been bugged seemed sufficiently real to make us move to somewhere we could be sure no-one could eavesdrop on what I soon realised were very sensitive discussions.

Much of my time was spent in preparing a memorandum on what I perceived would be the adverse economic consequences of the SEA on Ireland. I emphasized in that memorandum the new arrangements whereby, as a result of substituting qualified majority for unanimity on the EEC Council of Ministers, Ireland could no longer block decisions on "measures concerned with the protection of savings, in particular the granting of credit or the exercise of the banking profession". I emphasized how that appeared to breach flagrantly Article

119

45.2.IV of the Constitution: "that in what pertains to the control of credit, the constant and predominant aim shall be the welfare of the people as a whole". My other role during those hectic post-Christmas days was "gofor" – go for this document, go for that book, or go for that pot of tea, which the assembled lawyers needed as they worked each day into the small hours of the next morning.

I had by now begun to realise why litigation is so infernally expensive. A lawyer in court sets out a case before a judge or judges who are at least as expert in the law as the lawyer. The judges, contrary to the popular view of their being semi-somnolent as the lawyer drones on, seemed to follow the case word by word. Every so often, they interjected a comment or a query. Nor were the lawyers on the other side loath similarly to intervene. Most of us could have dealt with the interventions had we a couple of weeks for research and contemplation. The lawyer, on his feet in the well of the court, has a couple of seconds in which to reply or fail to reply. Complete concentration is therefore necessary for presenting the case in court. But not only that; if one values one's reputation – and by the time one becomes a highly respected Senior Counsel, one values this very highly indeed – one makes sure that the case being presented is the best possible one, and that one is familiar with all of its ramifications.

The strain of preparing and presenting a case that created the legal precedent of blocking government in its law and treaty making functions and that simultaneously thwarted the plans of the governments of the other eleven EEC states was intolerable for one man. I had myself begun to find intolerable the strain of worrying if Paul Callan would break under the pressures that had been placed on him as the case proceeded. Immediately after Christmas, therefore, two more Senior Counsel, Aidan Browne and Eoin McGonigal were instructed.

As "gofor", I had a ringside seat in the fag-end days of 1986 while the Statement of Claim was being prepared. Hour after hour, day after day and always into the small hours of the following day these matters proceeded. In addition to the three Senior Counsel and the juniors, Antonia O'Callaghan and Seamas O'Tuathail, Mary Lenihan and Joe Noonan were there from Cork most of this time and brought along their law firm's specially programmed word-processor which was invaluable in preparing and easily amending successive drafts. Anthony Coughlan was always there imparting a proper sense of the urgency of the matter, and there was Muriel, his wife, who held firmly to the principle throughout those days that "Se capall na hoibre an bia", and kept us fed like fighting cocks. Brendan O'Connor frequently joined the working party, contributing closely argued, well-thought-out views on the most complex legal issues.

On the last day of 1986, with all the issues threshed out, Paul Callan commenced to dictate the final draft of the Statement of Claim. This again was an impressive intellectual performance. Hour after hour he dictated, building up what was to be a seventeen-page, cogent, comprehensive statement of how and why we thought the SEA was in breach of the Constitution. Several legal acquaintances have since assured me that Paul Callan's Statement of Claim would take its place, along with Judge Barrington's judgment on Christmas Eve, as a classic of its type in Irish legal records.

Late on New Year's Eve Aidan Browne jocosely observed to me that I still had a couple of hours in which to transfer the family home into my wife's name! Once the statement of claim was delivered, the die would be cast and I would be responsible for costs which it would take quite a few family homes to cover. I mumbled something about "in for a dime, in for a dollar", and "as well be hanged for a sheep as a lamb". The die was already cast.

Despite all the pressure, like Cinderella we did not get there by midnight. In fact, it was nearly 1 a.m. on 1st January 1987 before Antonia O'Callaghan, Seamus O'Tuathail and myself, tagging along as some sort of witness, reached the Chief State Solicitor's to deliver the Statement of Claim. With the layman's dread of the law, I feared that even if we were not all going to be turned into pumpkins, at least our seventeen page document, each line of which represented so much sweat and tears, would be turned into a scrap of waste paper. I feared that the Chief State Solicitor, standing on the niceties of the law, would send us packing for being an hour over the time allotted by Judge Barrington. Then I witnessed the human side of the legal system. The Chief State Solicitor was expecting the lawyers and instead of any legalistic rejection of a document presented beyond the deadline, accepted our Statement of Claim and tendered to its deliverers a warm tot that was very welcome on a frosty winter's night!

The parties to the case were summoned to the High Court on 8th January 1987 to have a date set for the hearing. Still out of term, proceedings were in mufti; but what was lost in court formality was now more than made up by the weight of legal talent present. Each side fielded its full team. For the state, Eoghan FitzSimons S.C. was now joined by John Cooke S.C. Also for the state was the doyen of the Irish Bar, T.K. Liston S.C., an octogenarian who is reputedly an all year round swimmer at the Forty Foot, and a formidable advocate whom I would much prefer to have for me than against me. They were assisted by James O'Reilly, B.L. On our side Paul Callan was joined on the barristers' benches by Aidan Browne, S.C. and Eoin McGonigal S.C, these continuing to be supported to an invaluable extent by Antonia O'Callaghan and Seamas O'Tuathail.

The President of the High Court, Mr. Justice Hamilton, who presided on that occasion, quickly settled that the case would commence hearing a week later, on 15th January. It would be heard before a Divisional Court of three judges rather than the single judge who normally hears High Court cases. A Divisional High Court had not sat in Ireland for several years previously.

It was clear that the Divisional Court would include the President and Justice Barrington who heard the injunction proceedings. We were left guessing who the third judge would be until Justice Carroll ascended the bench, now like the assembled lawyers in full legal garb, at the commencement of the substantive case on 15th January. The legal argument proceeded on the two remaining days of that week, the five days of the following week, and, after a break of two days to permit the President to deal with other urgent business, the three remaining days of the next week. For ten days the six Senior Counsel teased out for the three High Court judges the issue of the constitutionality of the SEA. The court at the end of the ten days hearing reserved its judgment, to be delivered after proper consideration on a future date.

The judgment on 12 February was a shock. My side had anticipated an unfavourable judgment, with Justice Barrington dissenting from the majority. We were prepared in that case for an appeal to the Supreme Court, as the state would also have appealed had the Court not given it a favourable judgment. But the judgment which Justice Barrington read on behalf of the Court was unexpected. It found that I had no *locus standi;* that is, that none of my constitutional rights had been infringed. Until they had been, I had no acceptable grounds for complaint. Ratification of the SEA could therefore proceed. Reading this 47 page judgment took Justice Barrington sixty-five minutes. It took the President, Justice Hamilton, five seconds to pronounce "I agree"; and another five seconds for Justice Carroll to repeat that phrase, disastrous for me but the clincher for the state. Ireland could now ratify the SEA and allow the course of EEC affairs to proceed on their way, serving the interest of those 320 million Europeans whose fate, we gathered, depended so greatly on it.

I was in shock, as was Biddy, my wife beside me. What I most clearly recollect of those moments is that, before the session began, I had been approached by a number of press, radio and television correspondents who arranged to interview me after the judgment, whichever way it went. I sat in the reporters' benches better to hear the judgment as it was read. As it concluded, the reporters disappeared one by one to file their reports. Biddy and I were alone on the bench; symbolically isolated, to bear together all the dreadful consequences of losing a horrendously costly piece of litigation.

I was barely conscious that Aidan Browne was arguing the case for our being allowed costs on the grounds that an important constitutional issue had been raised. The state, of course, disputed this application and somewhat vindictively, I thought, though presumably on state instructions, Mr. FitzSimons pressed for all the costs to be loaded exemplarily on me, as a discouragement to others from attempting to impede the state in the conduct of its business. The outcome of that argument, which was that the Court would make no judgment as to costs, barely registered and I did not realise then, nor subsequently enquire, what its implications were.

Whatever the fine print might say, Biddy and I were financially ruined, utterly ruined.

We had anticipated a 2-1 judgment against us. That would have allowed time for careful consideration of an appeal to the Supreme Court, which, we felt, would be more receptive to the broad constitutional issues being raised by the case. But we had not anticipated a unanimous, unfavourable verdict; or at least such a possibility had not been discussed with me. So far as I was concerned, when Justice Carroll added her "I agree", that was the end of the road.

But others thought differently. I had not noticed in my state of shock that Paul Callan had left the court, and so had Antonia O'Callaghan. Paul, it subsequently emerged, had correctly appraised, as it was delivered, the weakness of Justice Barrington's judgment on this occasion. Almost all the 47 pages of the judgment comprised a synopsis of the argument presented by both sides. There were only a few pages of reasoned appraisal of those arguments. It almost seemed as though Justice Barrington, through the very weakness of his judgment, with which the rest of the court concurred, was inviting us to appeal it to the Supreme Court where perhaps he felt we would get a more sympathetic hearing than from his colleagues in the Divisional Court. The weakness of the High Court's judgment delivered on 12th February, contrasting so remarkably with the firmness and erudition of the Christmas Eve judgment, invited an appeal and increased the prospects of success for that appeal.

Paul Callan had decided before the judgment was fully read, by himself and without consultation, that there were grounds for appeal to the Supreme Court. That appeal had to be initiated immediately, before the state could ratify the SEA by lifting the telephone to the Irish Embassy in Rome, where the instrument of ratification was waiting to be taken down the street for deposit in the Italian Foreign Ministry. For it was central to our legal position that once ratification of the treaty occurred, jurisdiction in relation to it would pass to the European Court of Justice, where the Irish Constitution had no standing. As I gathered together my bits and pieces of notes and the remains of my shattered wits when the High Court proceedings had ended, and as my erstwhile colleagues gathered in defeat in the well of the court, the news percolated through that Paul Callan and Antonia O'Callaghan were at that very moment before the Supreme Court.

It was, I suspect, something like the "kiss of life". Slowly my shock-numbed brain began to register; and as it did, the news came through that Chief Justice Finlay and two other Supreme Court judges had agreed to hear an application from Paul Callan that afternoon for a stay on the dismissal by the High Court of the injunction granted on Christmas Eve by Justice Barrington. I was sufficiently recovered to attend in the Supreme Court immediately after lunch to hear Paul Callan make his request for a stay to the Chief Justice, Justice McCarthy and Justice Hederman. The application was naturally opposed by the now familiar Mr. Liston. The Supreme Court, which I sensed was keen to look at the issues, quickly granted a stay to the dismissal of the High Court injunction until the following Tuesday, 17th February. We had survived to fight another day.

Now it was the turn of the state's legal minions to get their "comeuppance". Mr. Fogarty, head of the EEC Division in the Department of Foreign Affairs, and the legal counsellors of the various EEC Embassies had left the High Court that morning to report to their ministers and ambassadors that the saga of the SEA was over; the EEC could breathe again and get on with its business. Then they got word during their lunch-hour that the matter had got into the Supreme Court where there was to be a hearing that afternoon. And by 3 p.m. the position was once again transformed. Once more, everything was on hold. The decision which that morning appeared so decisive and final was back into the melting pot. We still had a Constitution, and - God bless them - Supreme Court judges to defend it.

A plenary hearing by the Supreme Court of an application for a stay on the lifting of the High Court injunction against the SEA was fixed for the Court's next working day, 17th February. That hearing continued for two days before Chief Justice Finlay, Justice Griffin, Justice McCarthy, Justice Henchy and Justice Hederman - the full bench, as is required in constitutional issues. It may possibly have been the ingrained snobbery which suggests that what's higher must be better, but I had a distinct impression that our case was getting a more receptive hearing in the Supreme Court than it had in the High Court. The questions from the bench appeared to be more penetrating and based on a clearer, firmer grasp of the issues. It quickly became evident that here were five judges who were aware that the buck stopped with them. If they erred, there was no one or nothing to undo that error. And what above all each of them was charged with was to uphold the citizen's rights under the Constitution. That Constitution is jealous of the rights won back by the people from an alien government and is understandably reluctant to surrender those regained rights to any other government, either a home-made Irish one or a supranational EEC one.

Our request for a continuation of the injunction against the government's lodging of the instrument of ratification of the SEA was granted and the date for the substantive hearing set for a week later, 25th February. At the very least, it was now clear that the SEA would not be ratified that month; and since it could not come into operation until the month after its final ratification, the earliest that could now happen would be April Fool's Day.

There followed a week of feverish preparation of our case for the Supreme Court. The hopeless unfairness of the procedure now became apparent. It was one thing to have a hunch that a piece of legislation was unconstitutional. It was another to build up a case that would convince a bench of judges and that would withstand attack by the best legal luminaries in the country. If the hunch were soundly based, it could be done; but only with time and a tightly controlled, disciplined team. These we did not have. A week in which to prepare for the Supreme Court a case of such remarkable complexity was derisory.

The scant time allowed to prepare our case added to the pressures on our lawyers. The leader, Paul Callan, had been working exclusively on the case since the beginning of December. Aidan Browne and Eoin McGonigle had joined after Christmas. All three, with the juniors Antonia O'Callaghan and Seamas O'Tuathail, had worked flat out preparing for and attending the hearing in the High Court for ten days. There had been an interlude at the beginning of February which allowed the lawyers to apprise themselves of other aspects of their lives; but from 12th February, when the High Court judgment was delivered, they were once more into the fray. Now, with a mere week to prepare the most complex constitutional case ever to go to the Supreme Court, nerves were stretched. These were by no means ideal conditions in which to work. But if the Supreme Court gave us a week to prepare our case, then a week it was.

The substantive hearing of the challenge to the constitutionality of the SEA was heard before the Supreme Court on 25th, 26th and 27th February and through the 2nd, 3rd and 4th March. Judgment was reserved and was delivered on 9th April.

The case, of course, was reported in the newspapers. It will become part of the country's legal lore. Two points remain particularly clear in my by no means faultless memory. Both involve Mr. Justice Walsh, who is possibly the best regarded constitutional lawyer in Ireland and who replaced Mr. Justice McCarthy on the bench of judges who had heard our request for a continuing injunction.

Mr. FitzSimons, for the state, lost no time in attacking our case on the grounds that were held against us in the High Court, that is, my lack of *locus standi*. The state's case was that I had suffered no personal loss from the SEA; and it would be time enough for me to seek to have the SEA struck down when I could point to such loss. This argument, which weighed heavily with the High Court, got shorter shrift in the Supreme Court where it was recognized that, once the SEA was ratified, I and every citizen would have lost the protection of the Constitution. Justice Walsh, I thought, put the matter of my *locus standi* well and wittily when, as I recollect, he observed to Mr. FitzSimons: "But wasn't Mr. Crotty the man with his finger in the dike when the Constitution was being washed away?"

While not on the bench of Supreme Court judges who heard our request for the continuing injunction in 17-18th February, Mr. Justice Walsh was heard from before the case was finished, pertaining to a matter that arose during that hearing. Eoghan FitzSimons, for the state, had read an affidavit on 18th February from Mr. Fogarty, the Head of the EEC Division of the Department of Foreign Affairs and later Irish Ambassador in Rome. The purport of that affidavit was to impress upon the court how very well Ireland had done, and was doing, from the EEC. These major benefits, on which the country greatly depended, did not so much derive from the inherent nature of the EEC, it was implied, but from the skill and diligence of successive Irish administrations in securing maximum benefit from the EEC. (An uncharitable view might have been that we had been more persistent and shameless in rattling the begging bowl.) The import of Mr. Fogarty's affidavit was that our good standing with the EEC should not be jeopardized by needless legal delays.

The *Irish Times* was running on those days a series dealing with the people outside the limelight who wielded power in Ireland. As luck had it, the contribution dealing with the Supreme Court appeared on 4th March, the last day of the hearing of the SEA case. The author of the series, Fergus Pyle, had interviewed Justice Walsh as the best regarded constitutional lawyer in the country. Instancing the sloth and incompetence of the legislative and executive branches of government and of their penchant for attributing the consequential delays to the procrastination of the judicial system, Justice Walsh referred to Mr. Fogarty's affidavit. The judge reminded the journalist, Mr. Pyle, that the heads of state and government of the EEC had agreed a year earlier, in February 1986, to ratify the SEA according to the Constitutional requirements of their respective countries so as to enable the measure to come into operation on 1st January, 1987. Yet the Irish government had done nothing between February and December 1986 to discharge their responsibilities in the matter. Now, a year later, a senior official of the government had the temerity to ask the Supreme Court to short-circuit its deliberations and give peremptory treatment to a citizen's appeal in defence of his constitutional rights.

It was encouraging to read this in the *Irish Times* on the final day of the hearing. Presumably Mr. Fitzsimons and Mr. Fogarty, who were both in court, had also read it, and I wondered if the matter would be raised. But apparently the State decided that one goof was enough and they let that dog sleep.

The encouragement we took from Justice Walsh's comments on Mr. Fogarty's plea for summary justice - as though anything could have been more precipitate than the preparation and presentation of this most complex case before the High Court and the Supreme Court within ten weeks - was, however, soon dissipated. By the time the Supreme Court's judgment was to be delivered, Biddy and I were bracing ourselves for defeat. There were many straws in the wind. Not the least foreboding of these was an assurance given the previous week by Brian Lenihan, the Tanaiste and Foreign Minister in the incoming Fianna Fail administration, to his fellow Foreign Ministers in the EEC, that the legal hiccup in Ireland over the SEA would soon be resolved; and that Ireland would no longer hold up Europe's progress. Mindful of the horrible moments on 12th February when the High Court had pronounced unanimously against us, Biddy decided to remain at home and suffer the oncoming blow in private.

The Supreme Court, when appraising the constitutionality of legislation, offers a single judgment only. That is understandable. It would be intolerable, for example, if a Bill was passed into law by 84 TDs voting for it while 82 voted against, and was subsequently struck down by three Supreme Court judges while two judged it constitutional. When, therefore, Chief Justice Finlay gave judgment at noon that day that the European Communities Act bringing the SEA into our domestic law was not unconstitutional, the bottom dropped out of my world for the second time this year. Everything was lost: the case; all my material assets, which would not be nearly adequate to cover what I imagined the costs would be; and a good hunk of whatever reputation I had.

Scarcely comprehending, I heard and saw Chief Justice Finlay, having completed the reading of the judgment on the legislation implementing Titles I and II of the SEA, proceed to read from another judgment. As he read, it dawned on me that he was now dealing with Title III of the Single European Act. This was, so to speak, the second leg of the SEA. The first leg, Titles I and II, deals with amendments to the existing Treaty of Rome. Because this affects existing Irish legislation, it had itself to go through the full legislative procedure. The second leg of the SEA, Title III, was a major departure in foreign policy, a treaty which required endorsement by a Dail motion of approval but which did not require domestic legislation. Not an Act of the Oireachtas, on which there could only be a single Supreme Court verdict, without evidence of internal dissent among the judges, but a Dail motion was involved here. On that, as on all matters other than the constitutionality of legislation, the Supreme Court judges are required to give their individual judgments.

Half joking, wholly earnest, the point had been made to me from time to time during the preparation of our case that the least important concern in litigation was informing the plaintiff. It is like a complex medical case: the professionals have a challenging problem on their hands; they don't need the added distraction of keeping informed the poor blighter most concerned of how close or far he may be from the great divide. No one had troubled to explain these legal niceties to me.

By the time I had got them sorted out in my mind, Chief Justice Finlay had come to the end of his judgment on Title III of the SEA. This was to the effect that we had also failed to establish that this part of the SEA was unconstitutional, killing my hopes twice in the one day. This was rather like Mary McGuinness, an old retainer on the neighbouring farm in Dunbell. Dropping in one evening, I found Mary more garrulous than usual and enquired what was amiss. She explained: "There's an auld hen here. I kilt it this morning and it's not dead yet". Like Mary McGuinness's old hen, Chief Justice Finlay had killed my hope when he read the Court's judgment on Titles I and II of the SEA; and he proceeded to kill it again when he went on to give his judgment on Title III.

Justice Walsh had now commenced to read his judgment and hope, like Mary McGuinness's old hen, refused to die. I began at last to understand fully the procedure. All five judges were to deliver judgments on the constitutionality of Title III. All I needed was one of those four remaining judges to find in my favour and all might not yet be lost

Once embarked on the case, it had become a question of all or nothing. There had never, since the lodging of the Statement of Claim at 1 a.m. on New Year's Day, been any question of withdrawing before the full litigation process had been exhausted. As well be hanged for a sheep as a lamb. For months the adrenalin had run and, apart from the hour when the High Court judgment was delivered and one or two bad moments in the small hours of the morning, I had not reckoned the cost until Chief Justice Finlay registered his judgment. Then the whole awesome weight of it bore me down. Biddy and I would be pauperized. No matter how long we lived, neither of us could hope to escape the burden of debt that had been incurred by the court case. But now, as for the first time I confronted fully that reality, a chink of hope also appeared.

If one of the four remaining judges found in my favour, then there was the possibility that the Court might not award the state's legal expenses against me. That was a somewhat academic point, as all it implied would be that the state's lawyers would not be joining my own lawyers in picking over the Crotty assets, which were quite inadequate to cover the costs of even one legal team. But more: I now knew enough about the working of the legal system to realise that a single favourable judgment might cause the court to decide that I had a "fair point in law"; that I was not merely "the litigious person, the crank, the obstructionist, the meddlesome, the perverse, the officious man of straw", as Mr. Justice Henchy had put it in the case of *Cahill v Sutton*. The court might accept that I was a reasonable citizen, not merely exercizing rights, but fulfilling a duty to uphold and defend the Constitution. In that case I might even be awarded costs.

Justice Walsh had got well into his judgment by the time I had figured out these matters. Here indeed was hope, and confirmation of how reasonable people, even expert people, can study the same issue and arrive at quite different conclusions.

> Two men looked through prison bars,
> One saw mud and the other saw stars.

It was clear from an early stage of the reading that Justice Walsh's judgment was going to be in my favour. A few moments earlier, I had been engulfed in despair. Now there was a glimmer of hope. Perhaps I might yet escape from this court, having fought and lost a good fight as I saw it, without having to pay an impossible price for doing so.

Justice Griffin's judgment followed Justice Walsh's. He concurred with the Chief Justice in finding against us on Title

III. Two to one against and two to go.

Then Justice Henchy began to read his judgment. He had been the unknown quantity during the case. I had marked the Chief Justice as unsympathetic. Justice Walsh was the oldest justice on the bench, renowned for his several distinguished contributions to that evolution of Irish constitutional law which had been initiated by Justice Cearbhall O'Dalaigh. I had confidence that Justice Walsh's judgment would be wide-ranging and would give due regard to all the issues; that it would be a good and perhaps not unfavourable judgment. Justice Griffin's touch was much lighter than Justice Finlay's; somewhat mercurial but on the whole not running in my favour. His unfavourable judgment was not unexpected. But how would the Henchy judgment go?

When all is at stake one watches every gesture of the judges from the moment the usher announces their ascent to the bench at the beginning of the day's proceedings until their departure in the late afternoon. And one did this day after day through the six days that the SEA case lasted in the Supreme Court. Justice Henchy's attitude was the most difficult to determine. Justices Finlay and Justice Griffin I had marked, from the timing, nature and delivery of their questions and observations, as not favourably disposed towards my view of the SEA. Justices Walsh and Hederman by the same token I had divined as well disposed. Justice Henchy was the unknown factor among the judges. His questions and comments were if anything more frequent and pertinent than those of the remainder of the bench. At one time these seemed to reflect an underlying, critical attitude. At another one sensed that his disposition was not unfavourable.

Thirty minutes earlier, after the Chief Justice's judgment, I had been in despair. Then Justice Walsh's favourable judgment had removed the threat of being clobbered with two sets of legal expenses running into amounts which I could not repay in several lifetimes, and had raised the possibility that the state might cover all the costs. But if Justice Henchy's judgment was favourable there was a more than even money chance that Justice Hederman's would also be favourable. Not disastrous, overwhelming defeat but, as Justice Henchy's judgment unfolded page by page, the possibility, the prospect, the sweet scent of victory.

Justice Henchy completed his favourable judgment. Two against, two for, me. Now all depended on Mr. Justice Hederman. He disposed of the matter quickly in a 200-word judgment read in two minutes. By a majority of 3 to 2, the Supreme Court had found that Title III of the SEA was unconstitutional. From the most despairing moment of my life after Chief Justice Finlay's unfavourable opening, which I thought at the time to be the final word on the matter, to the brightest, most exciting, most fulfilling, moment at the successful conclusion of almost four months litigation in the highest courts of the land! All within an hour. It was quite a morning.

The Supreme Court had found our politicians with their hands in the till of the people's constitutional rights, which they had been attempting to filch.

Much was made by the establishment subsequently of the fact that only three Supreme Court judges out of five found part of the SEA, Title III, to be unconstitutional. Critics of the judgment chose to ignore that the single majority verdict dealing with Oireachtas legislation covering Titles I and II of the SEA, which had been read by the Chief Justice as the judgment of the Court, was widely rumoured to have represented the views of only three judges. In accordance with Supreme Court procedure, the dissenting minority views of two judges on the Oireachtas legislation on Titles I and II of the SEA could not be expressed. Only the dissenting views on Title III could be expressed.

Much of the credit for having the SEA struck down over Title III was due to Mary Lenihan and Joe Noonan who had submitted a wide-ranging and penetrating memorandum on the subject. That memorandum had been the basis of the challenge to Title III.

That the Supreme Court did not find Titles I and II of the SEA unconstitutional was disappointing though not really surprising. The case had been run on a shoestring, with few resources and very little time. Paul Callan, the leading counsel, had been under enormous strain for months and had suffered a collapse at Christmas-time from which he did not fully recover for the duration of the case. One consequence of this was that the economic implications and especially those pertaining to "measures concerned with the protection of savings, in particular the granting of credit and the exercise of the banking profession" had not, I felt, been put with adequate force and clarity to the Court. In particular, we had failed to bring out what I perceived to be the clear conflict between the SEA's provision with regard to credit and those of the Constitution: 'The State shall, in particular, direct its policy towards securing that in what pertains to the control of credit the constant and predominant aim shall be the welfare of the people as a whole". The SEA transfers the control of credit to the EEC, which is likely to exercise that control in ways that have little regard for the welfare of the Irish people as a whole.

Our legal team were required to go through all stages of a most complex constitutional case, from the initial injunction to the final Supreme Court appeal, in a period of less than four months. The resulting intolerable pressures damaged our case. Various other aspects of the Title II provisions had not been dealt with comprehensively either. These included majority voting, institutional changes to the EEC, fundamental rights implications and a number of other economic matters apart from banking and credit. In retrospect, under the circumstances that was inevitable.

The Court's findings on Titles I and II of the SEA were similar to a Scottish court's finding of "not proven". That is, we had not proven that Titles I and II were unconstitutional. This, of course, is different from a judgment that they were constitutional. The court decision in my case did not rule out a constitutional challenge to Titles I and II of the SEA at a later date, though it certainly lessened the chance of success of such a challenge. The subsequent amendment to the Constitution altered that position.

CHAPTER 7

Appeal to the People

An About Turn

The highest court in the land, the Supreme Court, delivered its judgment on the SEA on 9th April 1987. That ended the litigation and put the matter back clearly into the realm of politics.

The political situation had meanwhile changed. In December Mr. Haughey had been Leader of the Opposition in Dail Eireann. In April he was Taoiseach. Mr. Haughey in opposition had said in the Dail on 9th December:

It is dishonest and misleading for the Taoiseach, Government Ministers or anyone else to attempt to put the ratification of this Single European Act across as something of great benefit to the people of this country because that is not, in fact, the case. Many people are deeply concerned about the implications of the Single European Act for the protection of the fundamental rights recognized in the Irish Constitution. A clear case has been made, and the Government have not answered it. The proposed changes in the procedure of the Council of Ministers which permit voting by qualified majority rather than by unanimity on certain matters covered by the Treaty, without doubt are to our disadvantage and put us in a position where we will certainly not be able to defend our interests from as strong a base as we can now do... The Government's claim that the Single European Act protects and recognises Irish neutrality for the first time cannot be sustained. On the contrary, it commits us to a position of closer cooperation on questions of European Security, and that term "Security" is unqualified in any way and presumably is used in the same manner as in Clause 6c where there is reference to closer cooperation in the field of security within the WEU and NATO. It seems likely that there will be increased pressure on us in the future to co-ordinate on all aspects of security including the military ones. We must have misgivings about the completion of the Common Market. Our economy in its present weakened and depressed state is vulnerable to competition, especially unrestricted competition from powerful cartels in Europe. The Single European Act offers no special safeguards, even of a transitional kind.

So spoke Mr. Haughey to Dail Eireann in December 1986. In April 1987 he said to the Dail:

We have a responsibility to our partners in the Community to take expeditious steps to enable the Single Act to come into force... After we have held up the rest of the Community for several months, it would be unacceptable for us to adopt a dilatory approach... We cannot now reopen an agreement negotiated, signed in good faith and passed by this House without causing disruption in the Communities and doing damage to our reputation and to our vital interests.

This *volte face* was maintained by Fianna Fail throughout the subsequent campaign. Fianna Fail joined with the other major parties in wrongfully maintaining, as in the above, that the SEA could not be renegotiated. It could have been renegotiated, and would have been had the outcome of the referendum been otherwise than it was. It might have been expected that Mr. Haughey and his government would welcome the Supreme Court's judgement as an opportunity to have the SEA renegotiated with the other EEC member states. The SEA would have virtually put *finis* to the Constitution, the fiftieth anniversary of which was being celebrated the month after the Supreme Court struck down the SEA as being in breach of it. That constitution was the creation and principal heritage of Eamon de Valera, the founder of the Fianna Fail party of which Mr. Haughey was leader.

The specific grounds on which the Court had struck down the SEA, the abandonment of an independent foreign policy which it entailed, were ones that should have weighed heavily with the once "slightly constitutional", "republican" Fianna Fail party. Ratification of the SEA implied the replacement of an Irish foreign policy by the foreign policy of a Community comprising, in addition to Greece and Ireland, all of the world's capitalist colonial powers. Subsequent events showed that these matters were indeed important for the rank and file members of the Fianna Fail party. They were less important for the party leader for whom other matters, and particularly the lust for power, weighed heavily.

A week, not to say four months, is a long time in politics. Had the Coalition government been still in power and Fianna Fail in opposition in April, subsequent events would probably have gone very differently. It is doubtful if Garret FitzGerald would have opted for a referendum to amend the Constitution. Given his record of failure on two referenda, this most enthusiastic and uncritical supporter of Irish membership of the EEC would have been much more likely to seek renegotiation of the SEA than to face almost certain defeat in a third referendum. To ensure that defeat, Mr. Haughey in opposition, would merely have had to repeat the tactics that defeated Garret FitzGerald and his divorce referendum a year earlier, that is merely to withhold Fianna Fail support for an amendment for which many in his party had no stomach. Obliteration of Dr. FitzGerald and his Fine Gael party would have been assured by such an ignominious defeat, heaped upon the accumulation of other coalition failures.

Had Mr. Haughey in office been consistent with Mr. Haughey in opposition on this as on several other major issues, he would have precipitated a challenge to the power for which he had blatantly lusted for so long. His possession of that power was tenuous, office having been secured by the casting vote of the Speaker of the Dail. A decision to opt for renegotiation of the SEA, rather than to seek to amend the Constitution to accommodate the treaty as it stood, would have been consistent with Mr. Haughey's pre-General Election position and would have been very acceptable to the rank and file of Fianna Fail party members. But it would have been opposed by Fine Gael, the Progressive Democrats and probably the Labour Party. Given Fianna Fail's minority in

Dail Eireann that opposition might easily have precipitated another General Election. Fianna Fail would virtually certainly have been defeated; and that would have been the end of Mr. Haughey's leadership of the party and the power which means so very much to him.

The political reality of the SEA was that, given the premises on which the Irish state was founded; given the values and principles that the four political parties, which between them controlled 95% of the seats of Dail Eireann, had upheld and advanced throughout their existence; given, so to speak, consistency with the course of Irish politics since 1922, the scope for manoeuvre in Irish politics had become tightly circumscribed. It was circumscribed by the utter failure of those politics over the sixty-five years of independence, which in April 1987 had become more obvious than ever before. Notwithstanding a ruinous rate of emigration, confined now largely to the brightest, the best and the most expensively educated of the Irish youth, and notwithstanding government deficit financing equivalent annually to 14% of GNP, a quarter of a million people were unemployed. And notwithstanding the government's attempts to control expenditure which had given rise to the disastrous levels of emigration and unemployment, the state was continuing headlong into a public debt that, relative to GNP, is already the largest in the world. Understandably no party or individual associated with that total political failure could command sufficient adherence to depart even slightly from the course dictated by the logic of the facts as they were.

The core central fact, which determines every move of the Irish political Establishment in 1987, is dependence. The Irish state is now absolutely dependent on the £1 billion which comes to it by way of EEC grants and subsidies of various sorts; and on the further £1 billion which the state can annually borrow abroad, mainly because of its being a member in good standing in the EEC. Given on the one hand the mountain of unemployment and on the other hand the precipice of financial collapse, there was no way forward other than to ensure, as far as possible, the continued flow of foreign grants and credit. Facing that reality Mr. Haughey, to retain the office of Taoiseach, had no alternative but to abandon his brave pre-election words about going for growth in the economy. The political realities forced him to introduce a Budget no different from that proposed by Fine Gael and subsequently to pursue as his own that party's programme of economic austerity. Because, like all the political parties associated with Irish politico-economic failure, Fianna Fail cannot command a majority in Dail Eireann but is hedged around by the realities of Ireland's complete economic dependence, Mr. Haughey in office ate his brave opposition words on the SEA and hastened to arrange a referendum that would enable Ireland to ratify it.

I had no illusions but that once in office Mr. Haughey would hasten, like any client, to fulfil the wishes of his foreign patrons. This realisation, however, hardly lessened the bitterness that having risked so much and endured so much worry and concern over the outcome of a horrendously expensive court action – and much more so, having imposed those risks, worries and concern on Biddy, my wife – the success improbably won by litigation was now to be taken away by the vagaries of party politics. There had been eight constitutional referenda since the adoption of the Constitution in 1937. The Constitution had itself been adopted following a plebiscite on 1st July, 1937. The pattern of voting in these referenda to amend the Constitution had been as in the table below.

Irish Referenda Results 1937-1986

Date	Purpose	% of Electorate Voting	% of Voters in Favour	% of Electorate in Favour
1937	Constitution	75.8	50.9	38.6
1959	P.R.	58.4	46.3	27.0
1969	P.R.	65.8	37.5	24.7
1972 (May)	EEC	70.9	82.4	58.4
1972 (Dec)	Position of Church	50.7	80.2	40.7
1978	Adoption	28.6	96.5	27.6
1983	Pro-life	54.6	66.9	36.5
1984	Vote for Non-Nationals	51.0	75.4	38.5
1986	Divorce	63.0	36.5	23.0

Attempts by government to amend the Constitution had been defeated on three previous occasions, in 1959, 1968 and in 1986. Two of these referenda had sought to scrap PR. They had been put to the people by Fianna Fail governments and had been opposed by the principal opposition parties, Fine Gael and Labour. The third, on divorce in 1986, had been put to the people by the Coalition Fine Gael and Labour government and had been supported by the Progressive Democrats. There was, however, considerable opposition to the referendum's proposal by elements within the Fine Gael party. The Fianna Fail party's official position was that it was neutral on the issue, but in reality it was "neutral in favour" of the status quo and against the proposed change. Though as a party it did not campaign actively against the amendment, several of its prominent members and TDs did.

The rather qualified support of the political parties for divorce encountered the unqualified opposition of the Catholic Church. Elements that had been deemed to be dormant or dead in the body politic surfaced to oppose the divorce amendment. Refuting the savants, the commentators in the media and the writers of the leading articles, I, along with an almost two thirds majority of the voters, had refused to amend the Constitution to make divorce possible.

These earlier defeats for government in referenda were no precedent for that on the SEA. When a referendum had been defeated in the past, it had been opposed by the opposition of the day in the Dail, as was the case in 1959 and 1968; or, as in 1986, the opposition was "neutral against" it, and the principal non-party political institution in the state, the Catholic Church, was opposed. On the SEA, the four establishment political parties were in favour.

Or at least three and a half of them were. The leadership of the Parliamentary Labour Party, i.e. those who had enjoyed the fruits of governmental office, supported the SEA. Rank and file members and a couple of the newly elected Labour Party TDs opposed it. A united Labour Party had opposed EEC entry in 1972.

The only political party opposition to the SEA was from the Workers Party and Sinn Fein. These parties between them had the support of some 5% of the voters in the General

Election of February 1987. The support of the extremist parties, with the policies of which I had little sympathy, was the kiss of death for the opposition to the SEA so far as the broad mass of Irish public opinion was concerned.

Given the support of the mainstream parties for the SEA and the opposition of the extremist parties to it, and without the opposition of the Church as had been the case with the divorce referendum, there was no prospect of defeating the amendment. The opponents of the SEA would do well to get as high a proportion of the votes as the opponents of the EEC got in 1972, that is 16.8%. There had on that occasion been ample time to inform the electorate of the issues involved. Now the political establishment was rushing through an amendment on a most complex matter in the minimum time permitted by law, a bare four weeks. This was being done, too, at a time of unprecedented economic depression, when people were alarmed and concerned above all to secure what was left and to avoid the hazards of the unknown. The only thing that operated in favour of the SEA's opponents was that the EEC itself was no longer, as it had been in 1972, an unknown. Fourteen years of membership had left few illusions among the Irish people about the EEC, about "the markets in Europe, jobs at home" and all the propaganda "jazz" which had had such a powerful influence in the 1972 referendum.

It was said that I had thwarted the wishes of 320 million Europeans. More truthfully I might have been said to have thwarted a few hundred European politicians and a few more thousand European bureaucrats. Few of the 320 million people in the EEC knew anything about the arcane proceedings in the Irish courts; and fewer still cared a hoot about their outcome. But now that the matter of the SEA, after a spell in the courts, had returned to the realm of politics, I was just one of the 320 million EEC citizens. Or, more specifically, I was an Irish elector who, with 2,427,913 others would now decide whether the Constitution would be ratified to accommodate the SEA; or whether the Irish government would be required to insist on the SEA being renegotiated by the twelve governments of the member countries with a view to bringing it into line with the Irish Constitution.

My position politically, which had no more and no less

significance than that of the other 2,427,913 on the voters' register, was that this treaty was another, though an important, milestone on the road to economic undevelopment and ultimate chaos which had been followed by successive Irish governments since 1922. It was the same route as had been followed by every government in every former capitalist colony since independence and has led to the misery and poverty that are now characteristic of the undeveloping Third World. It appeared useful to use the occasion of passing the milestone to attempt to insinuate a divergence between the leaders and the led. Refusal to pass the milestone would by no means ensure that the same path would not be subsequently returned to after a slight detour. But any gesture, even a symbolic delay at a milestone, could help to awaken, in a people enjoying Western World values, doubts and questions about the bona fides of the political establishment. The wider the gap that could be created between the people and the establishment, the more clearly the people would see the disasters into which their political leaders were taking the country, and the more willing the people might be to look for, and to adopt, alternative courses.

If an alternative course to that of economic undevelopment and ultimate chaos did not exist, it would have been pointless to protest against and to attempt to impede that course. One should shut up and eat one's bun. One should either clear out, leaving Ireland, like the other former capitalist colonies, to go to the devil unimpeded; or one should board the local gravy train and grab as much loot as possible for oneself. But while recognising the highly deterministic nature of social behaviour, so that while individuals may diverge, groups behave according to well established patterns, it is also possible to recognise key turning points in social evolution when new routes were adopted.

Such a turning point occurred some twelve thousand years ago in the Middle East. At that time people deliberately consigned back to the earth seeds that they had collected from plants, and became the world's first crop growers. There, too, more or less at the same time and in the same magical place, instead of slaughtering a mature female sheep, goat or heifer, the animal was deliberately bred with a view to producing a stream of future animals. Thus did man change from hunting and gathering to food production.

Another major turning point was some three thousand years ago in Central Western Europe, when individuals found the need and opportunity to refrain from consuming all that they produced and to use what they saved to make possible greater future production. Thus was the capitalist form of production initiated.

Much more recently, within the last two centuries and also in Central Western Europe, propertyless people were for the first time sufficiently relieved from the pressure of coping with immediate necessities to be able to contemplate the future. In that future they recognised that the children of biological families would consume all that they could ever possibly earn, prevent them from rising above a bare subsistence and, unlike in earlier European property-owning society, would not be available as free labour to operate their parents' capital. They therefore did what no people and no species had ever done: they artificially controlled their birth rate. In doing so, they made it possible for the wealth being produced by capitalism to be used to improve the quality rather than to increase the quantity of life.

These innovations, introduced by anonymous individuals under circumstances which made innovation both necessary and possible and usually in spite of, not because of, leaders, have together made it possible for the developing half of the world to contemplate a prospect of a world where all physical wants are satisfied. Innovation of a fundamental nature seemed now essential if Ireland was not to collapse into the chaos of capitalist colonial undevelopment. The innovation required in Ireland was as feasible as earlier epoch-making innovations had been. Though none among the 140 or so former capitalist colonies, containing half the world's population, had achieved it, there was a prospect that Ireland might yet break the mould of universal capitalist colonial undevelopment. That prospect arose especially from Ireland's being the only former capitalist colony with western values and aspirations and therefore with a sufficient awareness to recognize the need for, and the possibility of, innovation.

The prospect of achieving anything along these lines has for decades appeared to me to be by far the most important thing in life. I have subordinated every other interest to doing what I could to move people's ideas along these lines. But in a referendum on the SEA, these political views counted for no more than the views of any other person on the voter's register. To have attempted to obtrude my own views in the course of the referendum campaign would have been pointless and self-indulgent. To have urged rejection of the SEA on the same grounds as I opposed it myself would have given the establishment another opportunity to characterise the opponents of the SEA as cranks and loonies. Whereas in the legal process the individual's viewpoint is all, back in the political arena, where over two million voters are invited to answer "yes" or "no" to a specific question, something approaching a general will has to be sought.

The Constitutional Rights Campaign beavered away during the litigation from an office in St. Andrews Street, Dublin. Its principal task was to bring in the money without which a major court case could not be sustained on a day-to-day basis. This was done discreetly lest a more publicized campaign would antagonize the court and jeopardize the outcome of the case. Procuring the official transcripts of the court's proceedings was an example of the day-to-day costs involved. Tape-recording being impossible, it was essential for the lawyers to have these as the official record of what had transpired in court. A transcript of each day's proceedings costs £800. Thanks to the Trojan efforts of the CRC and the generous patriotism of those who responded to its appeals, these day-to-day costs of fighting the case were met and a small reserve accumulated. From the start it was intended that whatever funds were collected would be used primarily as a contribution to the legal costs, of which, however, there was never any prospect of meeting more than a small proportion had the case been lost. If perchance the case was won, then any funds collected would be used to fight a referendum.

In the event, the CRC had less than £6,000 left with which to fight the referendum. Another £10,000 had been already spent on the court case and could not be got back until a year or eighteen months later, which was the time it would take for the state to deal with the costs of the case. These we estimated would be around £250,000.

My dealings with the CRC were at arm's length during the litigation. Micheal O'Loingsigh, who was prominently associated with the Irish Sovereignty Movement, was vice-chairman and treasurer of the CRC and treasurer. He passed to me from time to time whatever funds he could collect to sustain the proceedings. With a successful verdict but following C.J. Haughey's U-turn in support of the SEA, it became necessary for the CRC to switch from raising funds for a court case to fighting for the rejection of the amendment that the political establishment was putting to the people in a referendum to be held on 26th May. I was pleased and honoured to accept the title of President of the newly motivated CRC, which now rented a referendum office in Molesworth Street. This was located between the premises of our opponents, the EEC, westwards and our opponents in Leinster House, eastwards, as if symbolically we were trying to keep them apart.

True to Irish form, the first item on the agenda was "the split". Throughout the court case, all sorts of people in all parts of the country had worked away quietly on getting things done and particularly on getting money together to keep the legal show on the road. But now these efforts were to be redoubled and brought into the glare of publicity in a changed political situation following the February General Election. Attitudes and associates became important. John Carvil, for example, had given the CRC the benefit of his considerable political experience, organisational skills, wide contacts and prestige among Fianna Fail followers. He had acted as joint secretary, with Grattan Healy, of the CRC. But once the SEA returned to the political arena of a referendum campaign, John was confronted by the Fianna Fail leadership with a choice of remaining publicly associated with the CRC or losing his position in the leadership of Young Fianna Fail and on the party's National Executive.

Family Solidarity people found it difficult to cooperate with persons whom they recognised as having been their opponents in the 1983 and 1986 referenda. And, of course, the antipathy was mutual. These difficulties also surfaced between the physical force and the peace groups; the central-planning and the market oriented viewpoints; and so on and so forth. One impassioned speaker of the left, at a very early rally in Cork city, encapsulated the dilemma: how was he to canvass people to vote "no" when he saw that already people from SPUC, Family Solidarity and Sinn Fein as well as known Fianna Fail and Fine Gael supporters were asking people to do the same thing? The message of course had to be: a "no" vote was wanted and no questions asked about motivation for it. Perhaps the nearest to a common denominator for all the disparate groups was a concern for basic democracy and for the Constitution.

The wisest thing that those opposed to the SEA did in relation to the referendum campaign was to recognize at a fairly early stage that more would be lost in attempting to pursue an unattainable organised unity than could ever be secured from such a unity. *Faute de mieux,* we accepted that all political flowers should bloom; that too much time or energy should not be lost in attempting to coordinate, much less to regulate, the actions and words of all those opposed to SEA. The resulting cacophony doubtless sounded to many discordant, not to say ludicrous in some respects. But it was the people, or the politically conscious elements of the people, who spoke. And when the people speak, they speak with many voices. Only the *uno duce* speaks with *una voce.*

I enjoyed the referendum campaign immensely. The absence of control or direction suited my somewhat anarchic, agnostic temperament. While holding the nominal position of President of the CRC, my services as a speaker, for what they were worth, were available to any group wishing to avail of them. When and where I spoke were merely matters of logistics. Being carless, I used CIE rail-rambler tickets for the five weeks of the referendum campaign. They were remarkably good value, enabling me to travel in comfort and at ease over all points of the rail network. This, despite all the railway cuts, continues to serve most major urban centres. In the course of the five weeks referendum campaign I travelled up, down and across the rail system several times, getting to know pretty well every halting place and every stretch of track on it.

I lived off the land during those travels, which cost me nothing other than the rail rambler tickets. Arriving at my destination I was met or quickly contacted by a representative of whichever local group had invited me to speak, and handed over to them the leaflets and posters which I usually brought with me from the CRC offices in Molesworth Street. I was then wined, dined, accommodated overnight if necessary – as it usually was – and sent on my way with a contribution towards the cost of the CRC's offices, together with payments for the leaflets and posters which I had brought with me. The weather and the season – mid-April to end of May – were ideal for the task. The countryside, of which I had seen too little in recent years, was beautiful. Everything was good, but best of all were the people.

During those late spring and early summer weeks, I reaped a rich harvest for the outlay of worry and effort of the preceding months. The country gloriously, spontaneously, freely and nobly responded to what I was attempting. In every town and district, individuals and small groups responded to the occasion. They contacted each other – Family Solidarity, CND, Sinn Fein, Irish Sovereignty Movement, trade unions, Fianna Fail party members, individuals who like myself were attached to no organisation – and took local initiatives. They had to; there was no one to advise, guide, help or finance them. At some stage they would contact either the Cork group centred around Joe Noonan and Mary Lenihan; or the Campaign for Irish Neutrality and Independence; or Cosain, the coalition of peace and Third World groups which had been assembled by Irish CND at its office in Baggot Street, Dublin; or the Constitutional Rights Campaign in Molesworth Street. Whoever they were, wherever they were, if they wanted me to speak to them, I did so if a schedule that quickly filled permitted. At the time it seemed as though for weeks on end I was speaking daily to innumerable groups throughout the country, but on reflection one realises the exercise was much more modest. The whole business was over in a little over four weeks. It was rarely possible to cover more than one venue any day. I usually spent Sundays at home. And of course given the highly informal, spontaneous nature of every aspect of the campaign to secure a "no" vote, there were the inevitable cock-ups. A meeting arranged for one venue had to be cancelled for some unforeseen, local reason, too late to allow another to be organized instead. That happened twice. All told, I suppose I spoke at no more than 25 meetings, attended on average by about 200 people – many more at some, many fewer at others – probably no more than 5000 people altogether, which is pretty small beer in these days of mass communication when more than a hundred times as many watch Gay Byrne on the *Late, Late Show*.

Small or great beer, for me the exercise was enormously stimulating and encouraging. At the CRC office in Molesworth Street, a succession of wonderful people – it would be invidious to mention some and tiresome to mention all the names – answered a battery of phones which some unknown hero had twisted arms to have installed at a couple of days notice. They dealt with enquiries on the spot; arranged and held press conferences; scheduled meetings for some dozen speakers, as well as myself; prepared, had printed-out and distributed some one million posters and leaflets; and somehow, somewhere got the money to pay for what had to be paid for – the telephone calls, the postage, the rail fares, material and machine time for the printing. I learned subsequently that it had all been done for less than £30,000.

Throughout the country all these wonderful people, very few of whom I had ever met previously, organized meetings, took care of me when I was with them, thanked me for what I had done, wished the referendum campaign success, urged me to persist in trying to save this poor but dearly loved country of ours. The whole experience was akin to what one understands to be a great patriotic upsurge. People rise above their immediate, individual concerns, which for a time are subordinated to the greater, wider good of the society to which each of us belongs. The political and social nature of man and woman kind predominates over selfish individualism. People's actions for a time are not determined by considerations of cost and benefit to themselves, but by what they perceive are the requirements of the moment for the common good.

One realizes on such an occasion how limited is the world of balance-sheets, profit and loss accounts, promotions, pensions and so forth. The mood was that of people giving their all for what they perceived was a good and noble cause – the preservation of our Irish identity, the preservation of our Constitution, of our freedom, and of our capacity to try, try and try again. It is the mood that has achieved everything that is wonderful in human history - as well, of course, as being responsible for the great catastrophes. It was an intoxicating, champagne mood in which I existed, as they say, "on a high" for four or five weeks.

Apart from going where and when I was directed by those who assumed and were accorded responsibility for running the referendum campaign, I also more or less said at the meetings what I was directed to say. Very many people had brought about the referendum on the SEA. I was one of them and by no means the least dispensable. Circumstances had rather fortuitously thrust me into the limelight. It was their, not my referendum; more strictly perhaps, it was Mr. Haughey's referendum. My task was to do whatever was possible to secure the highest possible "no" vote. I went where and when directed; and I said more or less what I was advised to say. I therefore steered away from, without denying, my own principally economic grounds for objecting to the SEA; indeed I tended to play down the economic aspects of the SEA. My colleagues were of the opinion that the issue to which most people were responding was neutrality and, especially along the east coast, possible nuclear involvement. It was impossible to know how sound this advice was; I deferred to it in part because of the tremendous effort these advisors had put into the legal challenge to the SEA and which they maintained now in prosecuting the referendum campaign. I deferred to their advice also because all of them had more experience in organising and directing political campaigns.

In retrospect, I regret failing to emphasize more what appeared to be the likely harmful economic effects of the SEA, and not having availed of the occasion to attack the political establishment for the dreadful economic mess which the country is in. But the implications, if any, of a different emphasis would have been marginal. After all, as mentioned, I did get to speak to a mere 5,000 people during the campaign and what I said to them did not much influence the outcome.

One questions in retrospect the usefulness of so much unstinted effort given so freely by so many wonderful people. The Big Battalions were for the SEA. Individuals could achieve little against these. In five weeks' campaigning I got to speak to perhaps 5,000 people. By contrast, in a *Late, Late Show* interview after the Supreme Court case, I spoke to perhaps one million viewers. I have found the impact of that single appearance on the *Late, Late Show* frightening. Innumerable people throughout the country have recognized me from that appearance and have spoken to me about what I said on that occasion. It was twenty minutes of peak viewing time; and before the referendum campaign proper commenced. Our side had absolutely no say in how this devastingly effective medium of communication operated throughout the campaign.

As I understand it, the law requires Radio Telefis Eireann to give a balanced presentation of both sides in a referendum: the case for a "no" vote equally with the case for a "yes" vote. RTE did appear to adhere to these terms of reference broadly speaking during the early stages of the campaign, much to the annoyance of the political establishment. The Director of Broadcasting was then reportedly called in, and reminded that 95% of Dail seats were held by persons in favour of the SEA, and that RTE's coverage should reflect that preponderance of Dail representation. Following that event there appeared to be a marked shift in RTE's treatment of the issues. I declined to participate in a *Today Tonight* show towards the end of the campaign because I felt that to do so would give an aura of balance to what was on that occasion an outrageously unbalanced presentation: a panel comprising four speakers in favour of the SEA, and one against.

RTE made some pretence at a balanced presentation of the issues in the early part of the campaign. But the national daily newspapers made no such effort. All of them were clearly committed to supporting the SEA. Several journalists told me of receiving, unprecedentedly, editorial directives to give a favourable presentation of the SEA case. Being busy campaigning at the time, it was impossible for me to monitor closely the cover given to SEA issues by the daily newspapers. One could only get impressions.

Those impressions were that of the four national dailies. The *Cork Examiner* and The *Irish Press* attempted most seriously to give a balanced account of the two sides of the issue. The *Irish Times*, while declaring itself in favour of the SEA, undertook to give a balanced presentation of both sides. It then proceeded to swamp the case against the SEA with massive coverage of the case in favour. This provoked me into attempting to see the Editor, Conor Brady, and when that failed into writing the following letter to him:

Sir,

The *Irish Times* of May 16th had some 440 square inches of space on the Single European Act. 420 of these were devoted to the case for and the balance of 20 gave the case against. It is very correct that the *Irish Times* should have a position – pro, contra or neutral – on the SEA. It is, I suggest, very incorrect for it to abuse its monopoly position as a national daily newspaper effectively to suppress the case against ratifying the SEA.

The case against ratifying the SEA is so powerful that it induced me, a professional economist of some years, to commit all I possess and more, without the slightest prospect of personal gain, to preventing its ratification. The Supreme Court has judged it unconstitutional. The highest tribunal, a referendum of the people, is now required, after a month's consideration, to judge a most complex issue which has been in the hands of our political masters for 15 months, and effectively to emasculate the Constitution in order to ratify the SEA. If there is to be a semblance of a reasoned democratic decision, it is imperative that the matter be presented in an impartial and even-handed manner to the people, most of whom, by all accounts, know nothing and care less about the SEA.

The Government has sought to prevent an impartial and even-handed presentation of the referendum issue by RTE by demanding 95 per cent of its coverage be in favour of a "Yes" vote. RTE, in rejecting that demand, has declared that it will adhere to its legal obligation to give equal cover to both sides in a referendum. The egregious abuse of the freedom of the press by the *Irish Times* to suppress the "No" and to elevate the "Yes" side of the SEA argument is the sort of conduct that evokes demands for legislation, such as applies to RTE, in order to ensure a reasonably balanced presentation of arguments on this and other issues.

Yours etc.,
Raymond Crotty

The SEA referendum campaign was the first test of the calibre of Mr. Brady, a former editor of the *Garda Review,* as editor of a national daily, a position to which he had been recently appointed. The articles of association of the *Irish Times* set out, among the paper's principal objectives:

> that special consideration shall be given to the reasonable representation of minority interests and divergent views;
>
> and
>
> that no interest group or party or sectional interest shall have, or appear to have, a majority.

Mr. Brady's editorial judgment during the referendum campaign can hardly be said to have been consistent with these admirable prescriptions of his paper.

The *Irish Independent,* unlike the *Irish Times,* did not even trouble to say it would attempt to give a balanced presentation. Throughout the campaign, it was flagrantly partisan.

Again impressionistically, one reflects on the contrasting conduct of the two dailies: The *Cork Examiner,* a regional oriented paper, subject to regional influences and apparently responding to these; The *Irish Independent,* the largest circulation daily newspaper in the country and flagship of a group controlled by a non-resident, multi-millionaire. One is powerfully reminded of Edmund Burke's speech at the impeachment of Warren Hastings before the House of Commons in 1786. Hastings had misused the wealth of England to secure even vaster wealth in India. Had he remained with that wealth in India, there would have been no problem, except for the unfortunate Indians, but Hastings had political ambitions in England, and was ready to use his plundered wealth to advance those ambitions. Burke, in his famous speech to Parliament on the occasion, expressed dread at the letting loose of "all the corrupt wealth of India, acquired by the oppression of that country, for the corruption of all the liberties of this ... Today, the Commons of Great Britain prosecute the delinquents of India. Tomorrow the delinquents of India may be the Commons of Great Britain".

Miss Marion Kehoe, in part fulfilment of the examination requirements for a degree in Communication Studies at the NIHE, Glasnevin, prepared a thesis, *The Single European Act: What it Said in the Papers*. She kindly showed me the results of her analysis of the 62 articles dealing with the SEA which appeared in two national dailies and two provincial weeklies on selected days during the referendum campaign. The dailies were the *Irish Independent* and the *Irish Times* and the days were the 6th, 16th and 20th May. The provincials were the *Enniscorthy Echo* and the *Midland Topic* and editions studied were those for the weeks ending 15th and 22th May. The 62 articles were categorized as pro-amendment, anti-amendment or neutral. The results were:

	Pro Amendment	Anti Amendment	Neutral	Total
Irish Independent	9	2	1	12
Irish Times	22	0	12	34
Enniscorthy Echo	4	1	1	6
Midland Topic	3	5	2	10

It is unlikely that a more exhaustive study of the coverage of the referendum campaign by the media, including RTE, would show a less biased treatment of the issue. This is the unacceptable face of Irish establishment democracy and freedom of expression, when that establishment feels itself challenged.

In the matter of referendum campaign tactics, I somewhat regret, as indicated already, not having emphasized more the economic implications of the SEA. A more substantial regret was my failure to activate the country's quarter million unemployed persons. This is the sector of Irish society with which I most closely identify.

They are the casualties of a corrupt, inequitable and inefficient socio-economic order which I have studied for decades. It is an order which I perceive to be irredeemable, and which I most earnestly hope to see destroyed and replaced by one which allows every person to secure in Ireland a livelihood as good as is available anywhere else in the world. The unemployed above all have least reason to support and most reason to destroy a regime that denies them a livelihood, inflicts unspeakable indignities on them and robs them of their entitlements as members of the nation.

Of course one knew that it is not the most downtrodden who are the most eager for change. The downtrodden are too drained of resources, or too anxious to get out from under, to be concerned about changing the system that treads on them. Indubitably the most horrendous feature of the more than usually harassing history of Ireland was the death by starvation of a million Irish people in the 1840s with scarcely a murmur of protest. The more depressed people are, the more tractable they become. The Irish unemployed have traditionally been doubly selected for ineffectualness: they were unable to get employment in an economy which, thanks to massive emigration, has usually experienced approximately full employment; and they hesitated to join that half of the Irish population stream that has normally emigrated. Traditionally therefore the unemployed have not been a force for change in Ireland. But there has been a major break with tradition. Because of the recently imposed barriers to the free flow of emigration from Ireland, most of the casualties of a corrupt, inequitable and inefficient socio-economic order can no longer leave. Very many of the country's 250,000 unemployed are among the best educated and most gifted people in the world.

These considerations made me anxious to mobilize the unemployed against the SEA, which will unquestionably add to their number and lessen even further the chances of those already unemployed securing employment. In mobilizing against the SEA, the unemployed would also be mobilizing and voting against the political establishment, those politicians and party policies which, since the state's foundation, have denied a livelihood to half the Irish people. A vote against the SEA by the unemployed and their dependants of voting age was by far the most productive thing they could have done on that 26th May.

Immediately the referendum campaign commenced, I tried to contact Noel Hodgins who heads the Darndale Unemployed Action Group, the best known of a number of similar groups which are emerging around Ireland. I had written to Noel a year earlier on another matter, but also related to unemployment. A meeting was arranged, though not as quickly as I would have liked.

I found Noel, whom I met in the Darndale Unemployment Action Group's office with an associate, pre-eminently pragmatic, and sceptical of the possibility of eliminating unemployment. He was particularly cautious of allowing himself and the people who had chosen him as their leader to be used as the ball in any political football match. That became particularly apparent when I enquired if a relationship similar to that between other groupings of unemployed persons in Dublin and elsewhere and the trade union movement obtained between the Darndale Unemployed Action Group and the trade unions. Noel vehemently asserted that no such relationship existed, and that he himself would have no part in any such relationship. He perceived the unions as "the cause of half of his associates being unemployed". It was a view with which I fully concurred.

Noel Hodgins and his associate listened carefully to what I had to say and made several penetrating comments. I wanted principally the endorsement of the Darndale Unemployment Action Group for the anti-SEA campaign. The most Noel was willing to concede was that he would place before his colleagues any written statement I had to make. If they approved of the statement then it might be sent, with the Darndale Unemployed Action Group's commendation, to the various other unemployed action groups coming into existence around the country. I prepared a statement which was considered and, with slight changes, approved of by the Darndale Group. The Group subsequently sent it to the other unemployed action groups with their commendation. But it all took time in a campaign where there was little time available. Unsurprisingly but disappointingly, the effects do not appear to have been substantial.

Some of us who were contending against the SEA were aggrieved by the conduct of the media, and by the bare-faced manner in which the resources of the state were used to influence people to vote as the political establishment wished. The Tanaiste, Mr. Lenihan, admitted in the Dail that the government had spent, from taxpayers'money, £1,700,000 on leaflets and £164,000 on media advertisement to influence, in the best banana republic fashion, the people's choice. That was about fifty times more money than the entire anti-SEA movement was able to mobilise by voluntary subscription. In addition, the Government Information Service was used to issue a constant stream of propaganda in favour of the SEA. RTE, the national press, and the government propaganda services were behaving true to form. Pillars of the undeveloping former capitalist colonial establishment, it was to be expected that, on this issue as on all major issues since the state's foundation, the media would condone and facilitate the process of undevelopment.

A final point on those months when I was what I had never been before and am unlikely to be again, a person of some public significance: I was overwhelmed by a great flow of mail. It was all supportive. A good share of it was from abroad and especially from Denmark. Much of the mail contained donations towards my expenses. There were cheques, often without covering letters or addresses, and in some cases for hundreds of pounds. All of these went into the Constitutional Rights Campaign funds, where they were badly needed and where they were used to the best possible effect. My wife was kept busy during this period replying on my behalf to all the kind people who wrote, as well as answering the calls of the very many who telephoned.

What I was doing might not be terribly effective. There was no prospect of its putting money into any individual's pocket. But clearly a great many people agreed and sympathized with what they perceived me to be about. Much of that goodwill appeared to stem from the disgust so many fine, ordinary Irish people have for the corruption, incompetence and inequity of the Establishment.

The referendum results were disappointing. The various

groupings, odds and sods of citizens who cared and who were opposed to the SEA, had organised house-to-house canvassing. Few had experience of such political canvassing. I had none and I could contribute nothing to these entirely spontaneous activities which were quite out of my hands. Having more enthusiasm than skill in these matters, our canvassers reported in from all parts of the country overwhelming opposition to the SEA. We had even begun to think the referendum might be defeated, when the results of a MORI opinion poll was published on 21st May. This showed a 2-1 majority in favour of the SEA, though also an exceptionally high proportion of "don't knows". That brought the more euphoric among us back to earth and prepared us for the poll results which became clear by mid-day on 27th May.

It was difficult to find consolation in the results. I had risked everything I possessed on a court case to prevent ratification of the SEA. The referendum secured that ratification. Insofar as the SEA vastly extended the scope of the EEC and therefore the precedence of the European Court of Justice over the Irish courts, the referendum might be said to have completed the subversion of the Constitution of 1937. Henceforth the European Court of Justice, not the Constitution, rules.

But there were some consolations. First, a higher proportion of the electorate, 56%, than in any referendum other than the 1978 one on adoption, told the main political parties that it was not prepared to play their silly game of amending the Constitution. Only 44% of the electorate troubled to vote. True, just 70% of the 44% who voted voted "yes" and only 30% voted "no". But this "yes" vote was well below the 82%, 82%, 97% and 75% of voters voting "yes" in earlier, successful referenda to amend the Constitution. Of the successful referenda, only the 1983 anti-abortion referendum had a lower proportion of "yes" votes – 70% – than the referendum on the SEA. Another way of looking at the referendum results is that while 1,264,278 people voted in May 1972 to join the EEC, only 755,425 people voted for the deeper involvement in the EEC which the SEA implies. This was so despite the appeals of the entire political establishment and the illegal expenditure by the state of £1.9 million on propaganda material. That was a 30% drop in the number voting for the EEC. In 1972, when the Labour Party opposed, only 211,891 persons voted against joining the EEC; this time round, when the leadership of the Parliamentary Labour Party joined the rest of the political establishment in supporting the SEA, 324,977 voted against it. That was a 50% increase in the number opposing the EEC.

The results of the referendum were a far cry from what Mr. McCartan, MEP, called "the massive approval of the Irish people". Mr. McCartan had earlier distinguished himself in the European Assembly by describing the Irish opponents of the EEC as Ayatollahs, Communists and other such unpleasant types. The former Taoiseach, Dr. FitzGerald, was closer to the mark when he referred apprehensively to "the scale of the minority vote on the Single European Act, even when the main parties were united in its favour".

The entire political establishment, with all the vast corrupting powers of the state at their disposal, together could only induce 30% of the electorate to amend the Constitution. Those of us who sought to defend the Constitution against its emasculation, without organization, without resources and without the time to acquire these, mustered 13% of the electorate in its defence. That 30% against 13% is a majority of sorts. This is the sort of majority that Lenin's adherents achieved in a fragmented Russian Communist Party which enabled the 20,000 or so of them to call themselves the "majority", or the "Bolshevik", party in a Russia of some 200 million people. It is the sort of majority that has conferred legality, though not legitimacy, on the Irish political establishment since the state's foundation.

For the state was brought into existence by a majority of a section of the whole. The Sinn Fein party which founded the new state won 65% of the votes cast in the Twenty-six Counties; but only 48% of the votes cast in Ireland in the 1918 General Election. By partitioning off one third of the Irish people, the state could muster a majority in its support among the other two thirds. But even then, the political parties that operated the state could secure that majority only after a further dichotomy of the people in the Twenty-six Counties. The less contented half of those people did not remain to vote in elections against the political parties which have ruined

Ireland; instead they voted with their feet by emigrating. Of the two-thirds of the Irish who are born in the Twenty-six Counties, one-third votes with their feet against the establishment and one-third is left to vote in Irish elections. Rarely did as many as three-quarters of that residual third vote in elections; and governments were normally formed with the support of representatives of half or less of those who did. Irish governments have thus legally governed because they have been voted for by a series of fractions: 2/3 x 1/2 x 3/4 x 1/2 = 1/8 of those born in Ireland and of voting age. The 7/8 of the Irish people who did not vote for the governments in power were in Northern Ireland, had emigrated, remained at home on polling-day, or voted for opposition parties. Thus Ireland's "majority" elected governments, though legally elected, have had about as much legitimacy as Lenin's Bolshevik party in Russia.

The legitimacy of a referendum which effectively removes the protection of a Constitution from the people of a former capitalist colony and places them under the jurisdiction of the court of a community of former capitalist colonial powers is even more questionable. The "majority" who voted away the Constitution was 30% of the electorate; which in turn was the half of those born in the Twenty-six Counties who have not emigrated; and who in turn were the two-thirds of all those living persons who were born in Ireland eighteen or more years ago. The "majority" who emasculated the Irish Constitution therefore were 30/100 x 1/2 x 2/3 = 10% of the Irish. And that 10% of the Irish were induced to destroy the Constitution by the exercise by the political establishment of all the corrupting powers of a state that is corrupt, inequitable and inefficient.

Good work was done in challenging the ratification of the SEA in order to secure the flow of external resources on which that establishment is now utterly dependent. The challenge helped to strip away the camouflage, revealing that after 65 years of corrupt, inequitable and inefficient government the establishment, with all its corrupting powers, could only muster 10% of the Irish to support it in a referendum. One way or another, it failed to get 90% of those born in Ireland eighteen or more years ago and still alive, to express their support for it. At the same time, another 4% of the Irish spontaneously sprang to the defence of the Constitution and of the nation.

Postscript

The challenge to the SEA has been overcome. The referendum is over. A Constitution that reflected Ireland's position as Europe's only former capitalist colony has been emasculated. It is a Constitution which, like similar constitutions in scores of other former capitalist colonies, would in any case hardly have survived the approaching confrontation between Ireland's western values and aspirations and its undeveloping, dependent Third World economy. That confrontation is inescapable now that the state's credit is virtually exhausted and emigration is no longer easy. Yet it is possible to hope that the events of those months, from Christmas 1986 to the following May, may have an enduring impact.

Those events served notice on the other members of the EEC that Ireland is different. Our politicians, diplomats and bureaucrats may protest that we are Europeans like the Belgians, the British, the Danes, the Dutch and so on, but the events from Christmas 1986 to May 1987 suggest otherwise. We are Europe's only former capitalist colony. Those events suggest, too, that however well the EEC replenishes the begging bowl that Mr. Fogarty and his ilk interminably rattle in Brussels, the Irish state may not be able to deliver. The politicians want one thing, the nation another. Any clarification of these matters that is achieved will be beneficial, for it slows progress down the path of dependency and undevelopment.

The referendum on the SEA was an opportunity to dissent from a state and a political establishment which, by the day, are more clearly perceived as the enemies of the nation. As the

161

consensus of the political parties which fought against the people in the May referendum persists and solidifies into a new Irish political institution, the breach between the people and the parties, between the nation and the state must widen. The state, and the political establishment which has controlled and operated it for 65 years, can only move further into the morass of dependency and undevelopment. For of the political establishment can it be said with even greater truth what Patrick Pearse wrote, at Christmas 1915, of those who had taken over the mantle of Parnell twenty-five years earlier:

> The men who have led Ireland for twenty-five years have done evil, and they are bankrupt. They are bankrupt in policy, bankrupt in credit, bankrupt now even in words. They have nothing to propose to Ireland, no way of wisdom, no counsel of courage. When they speak, they speak only untruth and blasphemy. Their utterances are no longer the utterances of men. They are the mumblings and gibberish of lost souls.

Those who have purported to lead the nation for the seventy years since Pearse have led it finally into the same blind alley of dependence and undevelopment as that which all the other former capitalist colonies which comprise the Third World occupy. Power-hungry people, concerned to strut for a moment on the stage of history, they have done whatever was necessary to get and to retain office. Then they allowed the inertia of office to carry them and the nation further down the road of undevelopment and dependency. And now theirs is the consensus of the bankruptcy of which Pearse wrote.

Not one of the 140 or so former capitalist colonies, which together contain nearly half the world's population and some of which have been independent for nearly two centuries, has escaped the heritage of capitalist colonialism. Well might it be deemed an immutable social law that countries that have been capitalist colonized undevelop perpetually. But people and the societies which they create are not mere atoms, slaves to the laws that bind them. People are free; free to shape their lives, to seek truth, love and beauty. There are occasions, rare in history though they have been, when people, acting freely and defying precedent, give new directions to their affairs. Objectively, an occasion of this nature exists in Ireland now.

Thanks to past emigration, the Irish have higher living standards and are better educated than the people of any other former capitalist colony. As the crisis heightens, with the exhaustion of the state's credit and the ending of easy emigration, people can be expected to react more positively than the Irish people did in the 1840s, and more positively than the illiterate, malnourished masses of the Third World react. Auguries of that reaction were the refusal of 70% of the electorate to consent to the emasculation of the Constitution in the May referendum, and the 324,977 good Irish people who said "no". The dissent manifested then must be built upon, broadened and heightened.

There are two principal ways to do this. One is to collaborate with the inescapable march of events to discredit further a state that is heir to the capitalist colonial administration that was established here to exploit the people and that is the enemy of the nation; and to discredit also those who control and operate that state in order to enjoy the privileges it creates through denying a livelihood to half the members of the nation. The other task is to make people aware that the human, natural and technical resources exist, once privilege and its associated disabilities are abandoned, to make it possible, easily and quickly, for all the Irish to get in Ireland a livelihood at least as good as is available elsewhere. When a few per cent more people withdraw their support from the political establishment and a few per cent more are persuaded of the need for, and the possibility of, fundamental change, then Ireland's long history of capitalist colonial dependence and undevelopment may end. A new era will then be possible where the nation's resources are used rationally, effectively and equitably for the benefit of all the members of the nation.

At a more personal level, the lawyers who argued my case in the High Court and the Supreme Court remain unpaid for their services at time of writing (end November 1987). All the accounts have not yet been submitted and certified as in order by the court's taxing master. What the final bill will be remains therefore a matter of conjecture, but it is likely to be around £250,000 for each side, or £500,000 in total. The taxpayer could have been spared that expense and Biddy and me much worry had the coalition government of Dr. FitzGerald held in 1986 the referendum on the SEA that was eventually held in 1987.

INDEX

165